D0560189

*AM I LIVING A SPIRITUAL LIFE?*

*Questions and Answers on Formative Spirituality*

By

SUSAN ANNETTE MUTO and ADRIAN VAN KAAM

FOREWORD

By

*Adrian van Kaam*

DIMENSION BOOKS
DENVILLE, NEW JERSEY 07834

First English Edition

Published by Dimension Books, Inc.

Denville, New Jersey, 07834


Imprimi Potest:     Rev. Philip J. Haggerty, C.S.Sp.
                    Provincial

Nihil Obstat:       Rev. William J. Winter, S.T.D.
                    Censor Librorum

Imprimatur:         Most Rev. Vincent M. Leonard, D.D.
                    Bishop of Pittsburgh

                    June, 1978


L.C.C.C.No. 78-61428
ISBN 0-87193-065-X

# CONTENTS

# FOREWORD

## By Adrian van Kaam

All people are called to discover the unique form God wants to give to their lives. For Christians this means that they have to find their unique life form in Christ. It is not only a question of gradually discovering the form my life has to take but of allowing my daily existence to be an answer to this call.

My deepest desire is to be someone unique who lasts forever. A secret yearning for eternity wells up from the core of my being. I seek something lasting amidst the transitoriness of my countless self expressions. What lasts is my spiritual or fundamental self. This core self is not of my own making; it is God's gift to me, not a gift that I have but the gift that I am. God first loved me into being as a new emergent self, unique on this earth. He lovingly continues to call me to the unique life form meant for me from eternity. I must answer this call to be myself by commitment and ongoing self formation, by a life that offers to God a wholehearted *Yes*. This *Yes* to the gift and burden of ongoing self formation is the foundation of my spiritual life.

For most of us the formative meaning of life only bit by bit reveals itself in the act of living. As I live in prayerful presence to what happens to me, in me and around me, slowly a certain direction may emerge. I see a line; a hidden consistency makes itself known. The more this direction clarifies itself, the more I become aware of what kind of self formation is in harmony with the heart of my existence.

In the center of my being, God keeps communicating to me in love which form he wants my life to take. He speaks mainly through the circumstances he allows in my life. This book wants to help each reader to remain in dialogue with this voice of the Lord. Its aim is to assist the reader in finding the thread that holds the events of life together in this graced disclosure of what God calls him to be. I am not forced to say *Yes* to this gift of disclosure. God's call in the life situation does not compel a response. He waits with infinite gentleness and patience for my answer.

The mystery of my unique life form cannot be found by means of a test or a clinical interview. The ultimate guide I have is the underlying consistency of my life and its harmony with scripture, Church doctrine, and the wisdom of the spiritual masters. When I increasingly discover who I am before God, my life becomes more consistent. In light of doctrine, the scriptures, traditional wisdom, and personal inspiration, I become increasingly able to realize what is the best option among the different life choices that confront me.

This book illustrates this path by reflections on the many questions people ask themselves while seeking their way in the situations they face in daily life. We hope these questions and answers will help the reader to be more in touch with himself and his own hidden calling. He may not always be able to defend his options with arguments that cannot be refuted by the rational mind. It may be impossible for others to understand that a choice I made can be right for me. It is only in the long run that a chain of inspired decisions may begin to make sense. They become meaningful in the total formative orientation that my emergent self begins to manifest. It is often only in retrospect that people discover the hidden consistency of the many seemingly disparate choices they made over a long period of time.

One condition for the ongoing discovery of the form my life should take in the eyes of God is the ability to distance myself from the circumstances in which I find myself or from the problems or tasks in which I am actually involved. I must grasp who I am called to be both in and beyond my actual life situation. The responses in this book to similar questions by fellow Christians may help the reader to gain this ability for distancing in service of deeper self formation. If there are apparent changes in my life, it is not because God's call has changed but because my knowledge of this call has expanded and deepened during the history of my self formation. Since I cannot know and enflesh my call at once, formation is ongoing; it is never achieved but forever being achieved.

To find the life form that best expresses the call of the Lord, I may have to go through the way of trial and error. Before I commit myself to an answer to the question any life situation poses, I have to ask what answer is really the best one for me. The necessity of wise questioning can lead to a crisis. All commitment evokes the fear of making a mistake. Because of this fear, I may get stuck in an excessively prolonged period of trial and error. In that case I may not come to an answer at all. The impulsive attempt to end the period of doubt prematurely by a sudden willful decision is worse.

Both excessive delay and impulsive decision may imply unfaithfulness to my unique life form. This book will present for the reader responses based on universal human experience so that he may neither delay his answer to the situation nor respond impulsively without sufficient prayerful reflection and the graced guidance of the Holy Spirit.

# ACKNOWLEDGMENTS

For her invaluable help in reading the manuscript and offering welcome corrections and additions to the text that drew out with further clarity its meaning, we thank our friend Mrs. John Otis Carney. Together with Mrs. Carney's contribution, we gratefully acknowledge the EN-VOY work done by the following students, research associates, and graduates of the Institute: Sr. Una Agnew, SSL; Sr. Elizabeth Berrigan, CSJ; Sr. Andree Bindewald, O. Carm; Sr. Goretti Blank, SDR; Rev. Ray P. Bomberger, SSJ; Sr. Claire Brissette, SSCh; Sr. Joan Michael Carboy, SSJ; Sr. Rosemarie Carfagna, OSU; Sr. Marie Chin, RSM; Rev. Charles Cummings, OCSO; Sr. Bernardine Dirkx, SSM; Sr. Regina Marie Dubickas, SSC; Sr. Martin de Porres Fernandes, OP; Sr. Marianne Flory, SCJ; Sr. Janice Fulmer, CSFN; Sr. Charlotte Girard, SCJ; Sr. Ellen Guerin, RSM; Sr. Mary Cecile Gunelson, CPPS; Sr. Sheila Harron, RSM; Sr. Maria del Carmen Hernandez, CCVI; Bro. Denis Hever, FMS; Sr. Mary Germaine Hustedde, PHJC; Sr. M. Sharon Iacobucci, CSSF; Sr. Jeanne Jezik, OSF; Sr. Carol Ann Jokerst, CCVI; Sr. Grace Jordan, SSL; Sr. Maureen Kelly, SSL; Rev. Paul Keyes; Sr. Marie Kruszewski, CSFN; Sr. Victoria Lane, OSM; Sr. Alice Laferriere, SASV; Sr. Therese Leckert, OP; Sr. Brenda Mary Lynch, SSND; Sr. Kathleen Lyons, CSJ; Sr. Mary McKay, CSJ; Sr. Lucille Meissen, CPPS; Sr. Mary Mester, RSM; Sr. Agatha Muggli, OSB; Sr. Gertrude Mulholland, SSIC; Sr. Marian Murray, SHG; Sr. Lillian Needham, SSJ; Rev. Harry Neely, OSA; Sr. Mairead O'Reardon, OSF; Sr. Gemma Pepera, CSFN; Sr. Kathleen Power, SSJ; Sr. Mary Price, SC; Rev. William Sheehan, OMI; Sr. Sarah Marie Sherman, RSM; Sr. Marcella Springer, SSJ; Sr. Kathleen Storms, SSND; Sr.

Celine Thames, FMI; Rev. James Thompson, OSA; Sr. Mary Fidelis Tracy, CDP; Sr. Jeanne Marie Ulica, OSF; Sr. Anita Viens, SSCH.

## PART ONE
## DEVELOPING A SPIRITUAL LIFE

# CONTENTS

# I

## AM I LEADING A SPIRITUAL LIFE?

\* \* \*

In leading a spiritual life, there are so many obstacles to avoid, so many conditions to fulfill, so much trust in God to maintain. What assurance is there that I am approaching God more closely and not merely deceiving myself?

\* \* \*

How easily we can slip into self satisfaction in our spiritual growth! I remember that morning after Mass and prayers when I had been so devout! My meditation flowed so smoothly! Surely a sign that I must be growing in the spiritual life. But later that morning I "bark" at my secretary without apologizing when I realize I am in the wrong. That makes me stop and think. If I were growing closer to God in prayer, would I not manifest the power of this growth more regularly in daily life?

There can be no complete assurance that we are approaching God more closely. However, reflection on the way we live can give us an indication of whether or not we are trying to develop a spiritual life or deluding ourselves.

Our Lord reminds us in the Gospel that we can tell a good tree from a bad by the fruit it produces. (Mt. 7:20) Keeping this text in mind, we can appraise our life by asking, does it bear fruit spiritually?

What I do in my life is an indicator of whether I live for God or for myself alone. If Christ, not I, is the center, one effect will be compassion for my neighbor. Neighbor means not just the person next door but the members of my family, students and co-workers, even strangers. At home with Christ, I feel more at one with others. They see in me a witness of God's love for them.

Despite my efforts I may fail time and again, but if I live for him, I can overlook these stumblings. With his help, love becomes the source of my spiritual life, the light of my service.

Growth is difficult to measure because it cannot be seen. At the start of each new season mother stores the clothing worn in the summer or fall just ended and brings out items for the season at hand. She exclaims with dismay that last season's clothing doesn't fit the children any more. Yet she was scarcely aware of how much they had grown during the months past.

What a surprise when I notice the ivy on my windowsill. On a Tuesday it may look like a struggling twig but when I water it on Friday I am surprised to see the beginning of several new leaves. Growth has occurred silently, imperceptibly.

The growth that can be seen by trousers that are too short or by a new leaf ready to open is apparent only after it has happened. Though we may speak loosely of seeing something grow before our eyes we are talking about what has happened as a result of growth rather than about the process of growth itself.

In both examples, there are certain conditions that have fostered the development we behold. For the children, balanced diet, freedom from illness, and like factors help them to grow; for the ivy plenty of sunlight, water and fresh air foster the blooming. Growth is a mysterious process that we can facilitate but not control.

Growth in the spiritual life is in some ways like the growth we experience in our bodies. In the life of the spirit too, certain conditions foster nearness to God, such as inner silence, fidelity to prayer, recollection, and ascetical practices. All of these efforts are lived out within the confines of daily life.

We may be aware of alterations in our life with God, for example, a movement toward more reposeful prayer, a dryness and absence of delight, a truer charity in relations with others. We may experience the mysteriousness of this growth and realize that no amount of desire, willing or manipulating can do more than prepare for the gift of unfolding.

Growth in the spiritual life occurs within. It cannot be felt or seen. We will never know with certainty that we are growing in the divine life. Uncertainty ought not to cause us anguish but should be an occasion for trust in him alone. He who sees my heart's desire, who loves me more than I love myself, will give me growth in his own way and time.

Unlike temperature, spirituality resists measurement. For example, my room feels frigid, so I consult the thermometer. Sixty degrees. I go back to my desk and try to study. Though the crackle of the radiator tells me that the heat is coming up, I still distract myself by returning to the thermometer. Sixty-five. Seventy. Now I feel comfortable; but all I had accomplished by consulting this device was to compound my uncomfortable feeling.

In fact, preoccupation with the progress I may or may not be making in the spiritual life can be a hindering rather than a facilitating factor. When I attempt to measure the degree of my spirituality, I become introspective. My "executive will," not the Divine Will, becomes central. I want to know how I am doing. The emphasis is on me, not on God. Spirituality is seen not as a gift but as a project. I look backwards to the ground I have covered and try to measure the distance already traversed.

The author of *The Cloud of Unknowing* tells us the opposite: Look ahead, he says, not back. See what we still lack not what we already have; this is the quickest way of gaining humility. Our whole life must be one of longing if we are to achieve union with God.

God wants us to take the simple reality of everyday and believe in it. Spirituality is true if it emerges from the context of living in the daily situation as God's will for me. This everydayness, commonplace as it is, is the truest measure of the spiritual life.

Prayerful reflection is necessary so that we do not confuse growth with activity; intimacy with fantasy; openness to the Spirit with self-induced placidity.

In prayer we come to recognize Christ as the Source of our life. He radiates his mercy through our actions. Our life is his gift. Day by day we try to live in grateful awareness of this gift, letting each situation bring out a new opportunity for love.

During moments of meditation, we may not "feel" our rootedness in him. We may be unsure whether we have prayed or not, but Christ will dwell in our hearts, even in dryness.

To be on the way toward him is to live in faith even when I am not feeling, to obey his will even when everyday routine seems disappointing. The uncertainty I feel is precisely what calls me back to him again and again. Rather than become overly concerned with progress in the spiritual life, I choose to let this uncertainty be, understanding it as God's will for me at this time—as a message inviting me to return to his presence in faith.

An old priest was once asked the same question: "How do you know when you are coming closer to God?" He chuckled. "You know it when you are doing his will. You just know it."

"You just know it." His reply came without hesitation

and with the confidence of a lifetime of experience. He did not stop and think nor did he enter into a lengthy discussion. His simple answer reflects a personal understanding of the spiritual life, one that we, in our competitive, data-conscious world, tend to forget.

There are various ways of knowing, and the knowledge of intellectual certitude, of logical, cause-effect principles fails when we use mere techniques to evaluate our relationship with God.

The phrase "coming closer to God" means "becoming aware of God," for we are already close to him. St. Paul tells us, " . . . he is not really far from any of us, since it is in him that we live, and move, and exist . . . " (Ac. 17:27-28) Becoming a more spiritual person means becoming aware of our rootedness in God, of our dependence on him for every breath we take, every thought we have.

Daily concerns draw our attention away from this reality. We have to prepare classes, plan meals, look after business and family dealings. But behind and supporting all of these involvements is the spiritual reality: these people, events, and things are maintained in their existence by a loving, caring Father. Since the immediacy of daily life tends to hold our full attention, we need to increase our awareness of Christ's presence, of his secret plan behind all human projects.

The effort is not easy. Only the "little ones of God" seem to be graced with an ability to be busy with daily cares while fully attentive to God's presence. The rest of us are usually totally absorbed by immediate involvements. Thus to set aside special times each day, each month, each year to recollect ourselves in meditation and reflective reading is our only alternative. Such times help us grow attentive to his loving will. We become more aware of the closeness that is already there.

Gradually our fidelity to these exercises moves us closer

to a life in tune with God's will. Although our daily involvements still demand attention, they are no longer isolated and fragmented. In them we see God's love for us *and* an opportunity to grow in loving response to him. The people we serve, the dreams we dream, the relaxed and anxious moments we have still remain in the foreground of our experience; but we can, with God's grace, see them in a new light.

This encounter of the soul and God is comparable to the mutual loving awareness of bride and groom. As they plan their life together, the values, preferences, and interests of each form the backdrop against which both make decisions that are mutually beneficial.

God, far more than any earthly love, wills our good. He is the source and support of our whole life. He is always close to us, closer than we can imagine. We need only to become attentive to this closeness, given to us gratuitously. Our "Yes" to this gift is the measure of spiritual becoming.

## II

## *LISTENING TO OUR LIFE CALL*

\* \* \*

If our life call comes from God, how can we discern it? Is it a matter of listening to him speaking in the depths of our soul and responding to this grace? What if we refuse to follow this directive?

\* \* \*

When I have to make a decision, especially a serious one, I consult others whose knowledge and experience exceed my own. To discover God's will also implies an openness to what others can tell me. Choosing my calling depends not only on self and God, but also on God speaking in my situation.

Others who know me and my history thus far may be able to help me decide if my judgment is sound. Relying only on my own perception to appraise my life direction may not be the wisest move.

For example, a girl may apply for entrance to a religious community convinced that she is responding to her calling. After much testing, consultation, and guidance, the directress of vocations sees that she is better suited for celibate life in the world, or perhaps for the married life. This judgment is not an indictment of failure but a response to facts. The call to holiness can be concretized in a variety of forms and styles. Finding the right one is important and it may be wise to seek help. This person may truly be called to a life of intimate union with God but not necessarily in the religious state.

If the vocation directress believes this girl will not be happy in religious life, the only caring response is to tell her so. If the girl persists in believing that she should be allowed to enter, the directress still has the right to deny her this request and has the obligation to do so. She may not make her decision with absolute certainty; in fact she may suffer agonizing doubts, but, according to her insights into this person and the demands of religious living in this community, she must decide yes or no.

Not to decide is an evasion of responsibility. Since a religious vocation involves not just one person but a community and a shared future, it would be unrealistic for a vocation directress to say, "Do what you think is best. Who am I to disagree?"

In appraising the life direction, it is necessary to take into account the personality development of a man or woman; their degree of emotional stability; their ability to relate to other people; the quality of their prayer life; the balance they manifest of idealism and common sense; and such factors as health, talents, apostolic interests.

Such practical concerns do not deny that God may be directly inspiring or speaking to the person. But grace is usually given in line with one's unique nature, abilities and limitations. God works within the given structures of human life. We must respect these structures, which are his creation, and discern how grace builds upon them.

The school administrator, for example, looks at the position that has to be filled, the needs of the students, the existing faculty, the goals of the school, its policies and philosophy before interviewing applicants for an available position. He considers each one against the background of his particular school situation and only then selects the one who seems most compatible with the overall picture.

Like the administrator, the vocation counselor looks at the situation and makes the wisest decision. She is aware that the appeal to concretize the life call in some vocational form (married or celibate) comes from God and is usually in tune with what is humanly possible in one's life situation.

What counts most is the person's desire to live in intimacy with God, to live in the solitude, silence, prayer and reflection that prepares for and keeps alive this deep personal relationship. Next in line of importance is the physical, mental and psychological stability of the person. Standing on a solid foundation, one will be able to radiate a life of intimacy with Christ in the culture—in classroom or kitchen, hospital or parish.

The next decision regards the form in which to make specific the inmost call. Is it to be in married or single life? The life of a parish priest or that of celibate sharing in religious community?

The vocation counselor may not be able to answer all these questions, but she can help the person to assess her situation at present and prior to her desire to make a deeper commitment. For instance, if she wants to become a religious, a sufficient pre-entrance period will help her to see if there are any severe incompatibilities between her present life and the life she will be leading as a religious. At the end of the pre-entrance period, she prayerfully makes her decision—knowing that she is still dealing with mystery.

There is always an element of uncertainty, of mystery, in regard to the life call. For instance, if I desire to become a concert pianist, I have to find in myself not only a minimum of talent but also the willingness to devote myself to the discipline of practice and study.

There would be in me a spontaneous turning from other involvements toward those concerning music. If my playing consistently lacked life and understanding, if I rarely came prepared for lessons, if I showed annoyance at the slightest criticism, I would begin to wonder what "voice" I were hearing when I spoke of my desire to become a virtuoso.

Is my listening in tune with my life situation? Am I in touch with my abilities? Is there a strong enough desire in me to make the ideal of becoming a concert pianist a reality? Was the thought of fame simply an interesting fantasy I perpetuated about myself? What are the motivations underlying this professional "call"?

To find my vocation, I must search for signs in my present life that seem to point to that vocation. For example, how consistent is a person's desire for religious life with the way in which he lives in the world? One would hope to find evidence of an attraction to prayer, reflective living, and selfless service. Minor inconsistencies can be worked through but major ones may be irreconcilable with the aims and limits of religious life, despite what seems to be a person's "calling."

At the Last Supper Our Lord addressed these words to his disciples: "You did not choose me, nor I chose you; and I commissioned you to go out and to bear fruit . . . " (Jn. 15:16) Hence the question of who is called to the religious life and who is not is definitely the work of God. But how one responds to that call depends on his or her unique personality and the charism of the community one enters.

What is central in the life call is the invitation to personal holiness in the Lord; what is secondary involves how this call is made concrete.

My eagerness to listen to the call may blind me to my own limitations; hence it is helpful to find someone who can widen my view to cover sides of my personality I do not see myself.

We are often poor judges of our own situation; someone trained in vocational guidance can help us to see whether or not our call is from God or simply a self willed one, that is to say, one I have chosen and am determined to pursue no matter what the circumstances.

The person in question helps me to understand and evaluate what is central in my life. He or she assists me in discovering if I am truly called to married or celibate life in the world, in parish ministry, in religious community, and further if I am called by talent and interest to this or that professional commitment.

Because of this person's wisdom and life experience, she is usually able to take distance and look at things in a more objective way. Her responsibility is to help us discern, pray, observe and discuss what is best for us, keeping in mind the variety of channels in which God chooses each of us to carry out his will.

## III

### IN NEED OF SPIRITUAL DIRECTION

\* \* \*

Is spiritual direction a necessity to deepen religious living?
What can we do if we want a spiritual director but cannot
find one?

\* \* \*

When I start out on a journey to a place I have never
been I seek the best direction. I read maps, talk to people
who have been there before, arrange for places where I can
stop for food and rest. Once on the road, I trust that the
directions mapped out are correct.

It is possible to apply the same criteria to spiritual direction, namely, to seek help from an expert to guide me to
my spiritual destination. The wise traveller gets directions
before setting out on the journey. Similarly, help is needed
in religious living, especially in the beginning stages. But
the need does not stop there.

I may feel uncertain once I am on the road. Signposts
along the way may have been changed or removed, so the
chances of getting lost remain. I would like to find an experienced guide who is able to give me directions. But such
a person is not easily found. More often than not, I must
simply move on slowly but steadily, opening myself to such
available sources of information and inspiration as
spiritual books, conferences, liturgies, and scripture
readings.

Ultimately, all direction must flow from the Divine
Director, Christ himself. He chose to travel with us on this

journey to the Kingdom. Daily communication with Christ through prayer and reflective living is the surest means of finding and maintaining the spiritual direction of our lives.

Jesus himself has said: "I will not leave you orphans; I will come back to you . . . the Advocate, the Holy Spirit, whom the Father will send in my name, will teach you everything and remind you of all I have said to you. Peace I bequeath to you, my own peace I give you, a peace the world cannot give, this is my gift to you. Do not let your hearts be troubled or afraid." (Jn. 14:18, 26-27)

These words to the apostles at the Last Supper are meant to comfort all of us who want to live a spiritual life. They call attention to the essentials that we tend to forget in our day to day involvement in the world.

The influence of today's work-oriented society may hinder our efforts to live in union with God. We may be among the countless souls who are trying, despite the obstacles, to lead a spiritual life and who seek experts blessed by God with the special grace of giving direction either in private or to a group. The fact that these experts are few in number does not falsify Christ's promise not to leave us orphans.

Christ sends his Spirit to guide and direct the people of God through the Church. He told the disciples that he would not be with them in the same way he had been in the past. But he repeatedly says to them that they will not be alone, that the Holy Spirit will direct them, telling them what to say and do when the time comes. Also he promises them peace—not the world's kind of peace, that is, a sureness one can measure; not the security of having a clear plan of how to form his Church, but the promise of hearts that need not be troubled or afraid.

Like the early apostles, I keep looking for human assurance and security. I want to know how far along I am in my spiritual journey. Even if expert direction is not part of God's plan for me, I can trust in the direction I will receive from the Advocate he has sent. I find this direction in the details of my life situation, in the words of the people with whom I live and work, in the big and small events of my life, in the things that surround me.

The Spirit of Jesus as Master Director may include among these people and events at a particular time in my life the presence of a single individual to help me along. This is his decision, his design, an expression of his constant and faithful direction of me and my life.

After giving them his promise of peace, Christ tells the disciples not to worry, not to be afraid. He speaks these words to me as well. As an ordinary person, I join countless others struggling, with God's grace, to be responsive to his general, loving direction. Though I may never receive the blessing of a personal spiritual director, I can trust in the Spirit's guidance to illumine my attempts.

Growth in the life of the spirit entails dying to self as center and surrendering my life more completely into God's hands. The spiritual director focuses his attention on the Holy Spirit, hidden in the depths of the soul and at work in daily life. The director helps me to recognize and follow the inspirations of grace in order to be able to discern for myself what God's will is for me as a unique individual in this specific situation.

The aim of a good spiritual director is that I attain insight that will enable me to live on my own in trust and surrender to Christ, not to grow overly dependent on the director.

Knowing that Christ is my permanent director, I need not worry if I find myself without a competent guide. Christ may speak to me whether or not I find an experienced guide. If I am fortunate enough to have one, he may lead me through the ways of ascetical practice that help me to empty myself so that the love of God may suffuse my whole life. Through solitude and prayer, I learn to converse intimately with God. I also encounter him in the words of the liturgy, in scripture and the writings of spiritual masters.

Following these ways does not automatically make me a spiritual person, for intimacy with God is an infused gift of grace. I can only ready myself for this gift through these means. Readiness is marked by ardent faith and a deep hunger for the word of God. It also implies silencing the desires of my undisciplined vital and ego self in order to listen to the promptings of the Holy Spirit in my spirit and in my life situation.

This kind of listening is sustained by a disciplined presence to the holy words of scripture, Church fathers, liturgy and the masters. I have to put on the mind of one willing to be taught. I have to be docile to be a disciple. Patiently and carefully, I establish a relationship with the word by dwelling meditatively on what evokes a response in me—not grasping avidly for new knowledge as such but seeking to appropriate for myself God's message.

When deepening takes place, it does so within me alone. Grace is not a group experience but a solitary one, given in keeping with my unique human nature. The central focus of my life comes to be my presence to God in Christ. This is my lifelong pursuit. Since I usually do not have access to a person who can assist me in my spiritual unfolding, I have to be open to the broader spectrum of spiritual direction that is available in the example of other people, in talks, tapes and writings. The absence of a personal director calls for more initiative on my part and may foster a relative independence.

The one-to-one encounter between master and disciple is thus widened to include other relationships. From the example of parents, teachers and acquaintances, we learn more about how to pray and live a Christian life in our society. Conferences and sermons give us clues about following Christ. To profit from these opportunities for spiritual direction outside of the one-to-one relationship, certain attitudes are called for on our part. We must try to be open to whatever a teacher or an author says that resonates as meaningful for us. Then we experience the companionship and affirmation that comes from listening to others who have followed the same road.

Think of a fisherman's son who is learning his father's trade. He is directed by the elder man who warns him about the currents here, the shallows there, the signs in the sky that say seek shelter. Along with the wise experience of his elders, the young fisherman learns from personal experience about his own strength at the oar, how in rough seas and calm to know when he is rightly oriented and when he is off course. As he becomes an experienced fisherman, he will tell you that there are "roads" on the sea as clearly marked as roadways on the land.

The young fisherman is like the disciple setting out to deepen the spiritual dimension of his life. In the beginning, he must find another or others who know the course—that is, one who knows not just about prayer, reflection and the obstacles to spiritual living, but who knows these experiences from the inside—just as the old fisherman knows the treacherous rocks and concealed sandbanks that threaten to wreck his boat.

The disciple soon becomes sensitive himself to texts that touch his soul and direct him as surely as if they were a personal director. Because these texts address the universal conditions of spiritual deepening, he finds in them the personal line that guides his life. The danger to be watched is that one merely reads these books on shore, where he learns a lot about boating without ever really putting out to sea.

To man my own boat, I must learn to reflect on my life

alone and in dialogue with the teaching Church. One way of doing this is to keep a log or journal. To become aware of how I respond to situations helps me to stay in touch with my feelings, both major and minor ones, and to see their spiritual dimensions.

Writing is an aid to self direction, for expression helps me to become more aware of my self experience. As this inner direction grows clearer, I learn to move with or without the help of a personal director. As fishermen have stars or landmarks to follow, I discover from my journal of readings and personal reflections tried and trusted rules to travel by. In writing, I cultivate that inner compass of the spirit, which, if guided by the Holy Spirit, will find its way to God.

## IV

## CALMING DOWN TO DEEPEN SPIRITUAL LIFE

\* \* \*

Excessive tension is a signal that I have to calm down. A calmer life is generally good for you; is it also a sign of deepening in the spiritual life?

\* \* \*

One morning for no apparent reason, I find myself somewhat anxious and tense. Strange—I know of nothing that is upsetting me, yet a slight headache persists along with tension in my tummy, clammy hands, a stiff neck. What is going on? I mentally relive the last few days and come to the conclusion that I've been overly pressured, neglectful of prayer, sensitive to criticism. Many causes of tension have been piling up. I realize I have to calm down, admit these anxious feelings, and find their possible source. Only then can I feel at ease with them.

The way of coming to active calm thus begins with awareness of tension. After acknowledging that I am tense, I attempt by reflection to get in touch with the physical symptoms of tense muscles and a slight headache. As gentle reflection deepens, I seek the cause of this tension, for instance, too much pressure. I let these feelings surface and quietly befriend them.

As I try to understand my anxiety, I may get caught in an isolated concentration on self. Focusing on myself in order to root out the unpleasant feelings may make me at first more anxious and disappointed in my progress. I seem to become tenser than before.

This reflective approach does not take away the tension; rather it aims to integrate it into the whole of my unique yet limited life.

It is good to keep in mind that tension in itself is not undesirable. It can be a sign that my body is mobilizing itself to cope with an emergency. But tension is not appropriate when it becomes the usual mode out of which I respond to my day. A basic attitude of calm is helpful if I want to live a spiritual life.

What can I do when I discover that my stance in life is often marked by tension? A mere telling of self to calm down is at best a temporary and not too effective solution. Unless I get to the source of my tension and deal with that, I cannot hope to grow in an attitude of true calm.

Reflection on my tensions may point to a resistance to some side of my life that threatens to interfere with my projects, plans or expectations. Such resistance is often expressed in an "if only" attitude. "*If only* my boss would see things my way." "*If only* I didn't have that person to contend with." And so on, an endless litany of "if onlys" rather than facing up to the reality of daily life.

One means of growing in active calm is to cultivate a loving acceptance of the persons, events and things that enter unplanned or undesired into my life. Through prayer and recollected presence I am able gradually to surrender to the reality God allows. I can, in the words of C.S. Lewis, rejoice in its being so magnificently what it is.

To attain this contemplative attitude implies that I also accept the uncomfortable tensions that will most likely be with me all of my life.

If I am mowing the lawn, I have to make sure that the grass is cleared of sticks and rocks. So also in life. I have to try to clear away the obstacles that interfere with my attaining equanimity and begin to practice the gentling experience via a calming of the whole self, both mentally and physically.

A good way to begin is to allow myself to let go of all that interferes with my living in a relaxed way. I take note of my bodily posture throughout the day. Do I sit with fists clenched? Do I grind my teeth? Do I stand or sit with arms folded tightly across my chest? When I am listening to someone speak, or sitting alone in my room, am I in constant motion, frequently changing the position of my body? Do I feel I have to be on the go all the time?

If I answer yes to any of these questions, I may have to make an effort to help myself relax. When I find myself clenching my fists tightly, I can clench them even more fiercely and then consciously loosen them. Rather than standing rigidly with my arms crossed, I allow them to hang limply by my side. In listening to someone speak, I try to sit still and be attentive in a relaxed way. Just to sit and do nothing for a few minutes each day may also help me to calm down.

Active calm does not come all at once. Many of us live lives constantly on the move. We do not know how to say no to others. But what if we did? Would the whole school system collapse if we were to sit down for a moment? Some things are our responsibility, but there are many more tasks we become involved in without knowing why. We can't seem to let go and learn to take it easy.

A helpful exercise might be to look at my life and write down all the things I have to do. Then, beside each item, write the reasons why I have to do it. In taking inventory, I will see that there are many things I do that are not as necessary as I thought they were. Once I realize this, I have to let them go and resolve to put this intention into practice.

Being gentle and at ease can only come about slowly

with God's grace and my own willingness to be conditioned by that grace.

When I am more tense than necessary, I may notice that my vision narrows. I am unable to see what is really around me. When my head is bent intently over my books, my world becomes as small as my desk and chair. I do not see any further.

When I am worried about a particular person's response to something, that person may be the only one I see out of the whole group. Other people might just as well not be there. I see only the one from whom I expect opposition. When I am anxiously awaiting a certain letter from home, my other mail hardly affects me at all. My vision is narrowed, in each case, by my tense attitude. I am not present to anything beyond my immediate concern.

Calming down is facilitated by exercising my natural capacity to actually see what is around me. I must slow down and drink in what is there. Take a fresh look at my surroundings.

If I am beginning to live a spiritual life, I am becoming aware of my own existence as a restless heart reaching for the Infinite. It seems as if our life long condition in this world is a tension, a stretching forward to touch the unattainable.

As the food of God's word increases the hunger we feel for him, we pray that he will help us to become one of those whom Jesus calls his own.

An awareness of the infinite horizon opening all around me may terrify me instead of drawing me on. I try to distract myself from the truth, to obliterate the conscious thought of this call of the Infinite, but the strain of resistance makes me all the more tired and ill at ease.

My own resistance and refusal of the spirit is perhaps the deepest source of the tension that afflicts me and obscures the vision of eternity. The defenses I have built against the mysterious Other run so deep and are so much a part of my way of life that I cannot break free of their domination.

I experience ego desperation and know that it is only the touch of God's hand that can make the chains fall from my wrists. Only he can give effective power to any of my attempts to calm down the resistances that block out the inner call.

I can experiment on the level of human spirit with techniques of breath control and muscle relaxation; I can regulate my diet, physical exercise and rest periods; I can discover ways of distancing myself from business concerns without neglecting my duties; I can seek out moments of solitude and silence in which to open myself in contemplation to the presence of God.

Noble and worthwhile as these efforts are, conducive as they are to quiet, they do not of themselves produce the tranquility of spirit I seek. I must still acknowledge my helplessness before the Lord. The gentleness and peace in which I long to live must ultimately be found in utter surrender to him alone.

## V

## GROWING IN INNER SILENCE

\* \* \*

Silence is an essential of the spiritual life, yet many complain they cannot experience it either inwardly or outwardly. There is little we can do to change our noise polluted world, but can we develop interior silence?

\* \* \*

The increased noise levels of modern life are inevitable due to our technology and concentration in large cities; but noise in part seems to be a voluntary camouflage for our restless spirits, a distraction from the sense of alienation that accompanies accelerated change. It is bad enough living with the roar of buses and subways, drills ripping up concrete, fire and police sirens, but being bombarded by music, television and hard rock has brought many of us to an acute awareness of noise pollution.

Amid all this cacophony, we need to set aside times of quiet. Silence is not only something we must preserve if we want to welcome the Word; it is something that preserves us.

What is silence? To be silent is not merely to be mute. Spiritual silence is an emptying of self in order to make room for God. Ultimately it is only silence that can contain any direct experience of God.

How do we achieve this state of silence? It is a matter of patiently letting go of our controlling, ego ridden, manipulating selves. Willful forcing causes only more tension. Most of us have spent a lifetime focusing so intently on our projects that we cannot expect to yield quickly our grip on daily details and preconceived attitudes. We are like the westerner learning the art of archery from a Zen master. He could not relinquish his desire to hit the bull's eye.

With perseverance and God's grace, our silence will lead us to that solitude Franz Kafka wrote about in *The Great Wall of China:* "You do not need to leave your room. Remain sitting at your table and listen. Do not even listen, simply wait. Do not even wait, be quite still and solitary. The world will freely offer itself to you to be unmasked, it has no choice, it will roll in ecstasy at your feet."

At this point of emptiness we can turn to God who is waiting for us. This still point is found only in surrender, in daily dying, in letting go of our ego projects as ultimate. At the center of this solitude, we may experience a oneness with him.

Each time we retreat to a corner of silence in our project-oriented world, each time we practice surrender, we put ourselves in a state of peaceful readiness. We become docile. We come to know what T.S. Eliot meant when he wrote in *Four Quartets:* "I said to my soul, be still, and let the dark come upon you/ Which shall be the darkness of God." He concludes the poem with this reminder: "Quick now, here, now always—/A condition of complete simplicity/ (Costing not less than everything)."

As we learn to disperse these pockets of silence throughout our busy lives, we will slowly discover that work and action themselves are being transformed into pathways of prayer.

The words of Christ to the Samaritan woman come to mind:

"Believe me, woman, the hour is coming when you will worship the Father neither on this mountain nor in

Jerusalem. But the hour will come—in fact it is here already—when true worshipers will worship the Father in spirit and truth." (Jn. 4:21-23)  •

We know from this and other Gospel passages that Jesus condemned the legalism of the Pharisees, whose observance of the law for its own sake was interpreted as the sole sign of fidelity to God. In these words to the woman of Samaria, Christ implies that for them the exterior "where" of worship was more important than the interior "how." They honored the Lord with lip service, while their hearts were far from him. The inner "why" of spiritual living became blurred. In addressing the woman Christ calls for a renewal of heart, for worship rooted in inner dispositions, not merely in cultic rituals.

No rule in and by itself can lead us to the awareness of our personal need for silence. It is this need that should lead us to the decision to set aside times and places of silence in keeping with our situation in life.

Since body and soul form a unity, we cannot expect to acquire inner silence without at least some discipline of outer silence. Exterior silence is meant to be at the service of interior stilling. However, it is not wise to rely totally on external structures to enforce silence; it is the inner motivation that urges us on to the "still point" of our soul.

What happens without affects what happens within. In this sense outer silence lends itself to inner quieting. Similarly inward changes manifest themselves outwardly. Thus a deeper interior presence affects the spiritual quality of our outer activity.

Silence is not sterile. It gives birth to communion and communication. I bring to others what I have gleaned in quiet presence to God. Only through communion with him can I honestly communicate his message: "What I say to you in the dark, tell in the daylight; what you hear in whispers, proclaim from the housetops." (Mt. 10:27)

The best preparation for apostolic work is thus an atmosphere of silence: outer so that I can recollect myself before God and inner so I can listen and respond to his word.

## VI

## DIFFERENT APPROACHES TO THE SPIRITUAL LIFE

\* \* \*

Some people are oriented toward quiet prayer and savoring the word; others toward devotions and novenas. I am aware of the need for a flexible structure in spiritual exercises, but I wonder how this structure can evolve since persons approach the life of the spirit so differently.

\* \* \*

Picture a sturdy tree trunk with branches of all shapes and sizes spreading out in every direction. This image depicts one solid foundation with an outgrowth of individual elements reaching beyond the base but at the same time deeply embedded in it.

The trunk of the tree points to the basic treasury of spirituality from which we all draw. This treasury contains the essential elements of the spiritual life, such as prayer, periods of solitude and recollection, reading and reflecting on Holy Scripture and the works of spiritual masters, liturgical worship, and the sacraments. Without this foundation, there is little or no possibility for spiritual growth as a Christian.

The structures of prayer life should be broad enough to encompass these basic elements. The outgrowth of branches refers to the personal expression of the basics as lived by each individual or by groups of persons with like temperaments and interests. Some may find it spiritually enriching to share reflections on Holy Scripture. Others may want to express their devotion to Mary by recitation of the rosary. Still others may prefer mainly to share in the common liturgy of the Mass and sacraments, complemented by private prayer and spiritual reading.

We need thus to be deeply and personally rooted in the fundamentals of the spiritual life, aware and respectful of the uniqueness of each individual. Individuals, however, must not become too individualistic; they are after all members of a Christian community and should, therefore, be concerned about the spiritual growth and needs of others. If we provide room for one another to grow, we can each become the self God wants us to be.

The purpose of these structures and exercises is first of all to root us in the fundamentals of Christian spirituality, and, secondly, to promote the unique growth of each member within the community.

As children in a family come of age, their rooms begin to express more who they are as unique members of the family. In and through such expression, they come to increasing self discovery. Wise parents sense this need and allow their children a certain freedom within the boundaries of cleanliness and good order.

Despite the fact that their rooms are different, each member of the family respects the other's preferences. All work out their unique decor within the common elements of good taste, adequate lighting and heat, working space and comfort.

This same freedom of expression shows up in the life of prayer. The common element—quiet, attentive listening to God—stays the same, though expressions differ. One person seems to stress the importance of contemplative dwelling upon the word; another needs words in order to begin to pray and meditate. Both approaches, though different, are blessed by God. They can be combined in the same person. We often need prayers to find our way to a more contemplative presence.

At times I sit quite still before God to drink in and savor the experience of his word coming alive in me. The fullness of my being meets the fullness of Divine Reality. At other times I feel totally empty. I seem to be void of thoughts and responses—dry as dead bones. Unable to pray myself, I seek out formulated prayers and devotions, as well as bodily gestures and postures, in the hope that they will become prayers for me. Since I cannot pray, I let my body and these prayers "pray for me." They become the expression of what I am capable of offering now.

Within our personal prayer life, we run the gamut of experience. One day we need only to listen to feel spiritually enriched; the next we need formulated prayers and devotions. Whatever exercises we use, our aim is to keep alive the purpose of religious living—greater intimacy with the Divine Persons.

We have to be attuned to what is best for us spiritually today and flexible enough to seek it out. It would be wonderful to savor the word of God every time we pray. But each day we bring with us different joys and sufferings, attentiveness as well as tiredness, lightheartedness as well as lethargy. By being present to where we actually are and to what we feel, we can be flexible enough to seek out what exercise will best deepen our presence to God.

The same is true within the community. All of us are at different places within the range of experience. Because of these differences, a flexible structure of exercises is essential. If we have been flexible with ourselves, we will understand the importance of flexibility within community. No exercise can answer all needs at a given moment; thus a number of options are necessary.

Again the point that needs most to be clarified has to do

with the essential structures. If we look at what the great founders of religious communities required, we see that their concern centered on a few basic principles: the need for prayer, silence, spiritual reading, retreat. Through the years members added special devotions and favorite exercises to rules and customs—all of which helped to nourish the spiritual lives of religious but none of which are absolutely essential.

Time for prayer is essential, but a special prayer to a favored saint is non-essential. The prayer may be excellent for the person inspired to say it, but it is not essential that everyone in the community adopt the same devotion.

Although one may feel a deep awareness of God's presence when sitting quietly in the chapel, another may find that she has a sense of identity with Christ while making the Way of the Cross. What is a distraction for one may be an ideal exercise for another. The point is: both are praying. There is no need for one to participate in the other's devotions.

A problem arises if this individual approach leads to neglect of the fundamentals. For example, attendance at Mass and prescribed community prayers may be neglected in favor of making a special novena or participating in a prayer group. As long as caution is exercised in regard to essential conditions and community exercises, it is wise to respect the uniqueness of each person's prayer life.

What may speak to me in a scripture passage may not reach someone else. Our unique profile of strengths and failings makes for limitless possibilities of prayer. This diversity is as beautiful as that seen in nature. Yet this beauty often goes unnoticed because we are so close to it. Instead it becomes a source of conflict.

It may be advantageous that times and kinds of personal prayer are no longer detailed but have become the responsibility of each Christian. Just as each tree is unique and blossoms at its own pace, so each person's prayer life is a unique expression in the Lord of her personal emergence.

To impose one form of prayer on all members of a community would lead to impoverishment, both for the individuals concerned and the community as a whole.

Jesus reminds us that there are many mansions in his Father's house. The Father does not expect us to fit into the same mansion in the same way. He has allowed for variety and diversity in all manifestations of creation. He is aware that each of us has to go toward him at our own time and our own pace. He respects the uniqueness of each one's personal way. The question is, do I?

## VII

## LIVING IN REFLECTIVE MEDITATION

\* \* \*

Would you elaborate on the meaning of "meditative reflection"? Are there steps to the formation of this practice, especially for the priest, religious, and lay person?

\* \* \*

"I cannot meditate."
"I don't know how."
"It's not for me!"
How many times have we heard these familiar refrains. And yet . . . take a walk along an ocean front and there are many people, young and old, sitting on the rocks doing just that—meditating. They feel the necessity to withdraw to a quiet place, to set aside a time, if possible each day, to ponder the meaning of life and the direction it is taking.

This quiet place may be bedroom or basement, oceanside or mountain retreat, whatever facility is available and will foster an atmosphere of silence. Finding an outwardly quiet place is only a first step; it is necessary to grow quiet within, for no one can meditate when the mind is like Grand Central Station.

If our mind is in a frenzy, we will simply not be able to ponder reflectively. Difficult though it may be, quiet concentration and perhaps repetition of a sacred text, will lead to quietness of mind. Though distractions may disrupt the surface, deep inside we will experience calm waters. Gradually we will leave the outer tumult at the door and open our hearts to the words of the Father.

Meditation will not solve our problems; it won't free us from the monotony of daily chores or make our bad habits disappear all at once. But it will help us to face each new day with renewed faith and vigor. In a time of decision, it encourages us to discover who we are and to discern what God is asking of us. If we are able to reflect on the words of the Gospels in a meditative way, we will hear more personally Christ's message of love and salvation.

Meditative reflection unites our mind and soul to God; though we are alone in our quiet place, we are at one with him. And the closer we grow to him in meditation, the closer we grow to one another. We learn the true meaning of life and love.

In meditative reflection we see the whole self made in the image and likeness of God. By contrast, if we isolate a particular emotion, motive, or need, without seeing it in a wider perspective, we may get caught in introspection and begin to identify our whole self with only these limited aspects. Meditative reflection admits the whole picture; introspection only a portion, for it isolates our attitudes and responses.

The soil in which it is rooted gives the flower the strength to withstand the forces of nature. Likewise if I look at myself as rooted in the Sacred, I see that it is the Sacred who gives me strength. It is God who sustains my being and gives me life. If I cut myself off from him in introspective isolation, I lose touch with the healing presence of Christ.

Because I am human, I will fall; because I have been redeemed I am able to rise again. The joy of the Christian life is that we can continually become. Behind everything we try to see in faith a loving Father, who cares for us, who heals our past and transforms our future.

The incentive for living a life of meditative reflection must thus stem from a deep conviction that all that is bears signs of divine truth and love. This truth both reveals and conceals itself. In meditation we open ourselves to its revelation in a more conscious way.

Preparation for meditation can begin by trying to focus attention on something as mundane as the way we live some simple aspect of daily life. We can, for example, try to pick things up and lay them down, attentive to our approach. Am I sensitive and reverent in my openness to things or grasping and unfeeling? Can I modify my approach and hence spiritualize my touch spontaneously?

What happens in this example of attentiveness to how I use my hands can be applied to all events of life. I can see them as revelations of God's truth and love and appreciate them as pointers to his presence. I can learn to respect the many events of my life—the persons I meet and myself too—as gift. I can open myself to receive these gifts as expressions of God's generosity. Often I cannot fathom the disappointments and limitations in myself and others but somehow, if I believe that all that happens is part of God's direction, I can come to see the events of everyday in a different light. My view is not based on my expectations, imaginings, or desires but on the trust that all of life is under God's care.

To learn to reflect meditatively involves a gradual process that anyone can undertake. All that is required is that I regularly set aside some time to look at my situation in God's light. Slowly I begin to discover those self-centered, envious or negative outlooks that distort my view. With God's grace I can transform these obstacles and open myself more and more to the silent meaning behind all events.

I let go of plans, timetables, and projects, if only for a few moments. The words of the Magnificat come to mind: "The Lord has done marvels for me. Holy is his name." Whether I am a priest, minister, religious or lay person, I can quietly ask what are the "marvels" God works for me? In what simple ways has he manifested his concern?

He has granted me the knowledge of himself.

He has opened my heart to his Divine Presence, allowing me the joy of his peace.

He has eased my burdens with his yoke, giving me gentle lessons on how I am to live my life with love and in surrender to his will.

He has stilled my anxious worries.

He has comforted me in times of loss and pain.

He has made me aware of my relation to all creation.

He has given me a sense of infinite worth.

He has graced me with abundant life.

## VIII

### *SPIRITUAL READING AND PRESENCE TO GOD*

\* \* \*

How much time should I spend on the discipline of spiritual reading to make it fruitful? Does this reading affect my consciousness of God's indwelling presence throughout the day?

\* \* \*

A new awareness of the graciousness of God often threads its way through the day if we are faithful to the practice of spiritual reading. Even if we can only spend a minimum amount of time on this exercise, it can enable ordinary life to blossom with a host of new meanings.

The possibility of experiencing the touch of God in daily life is increased by the time we spend in spiritual reading. It seems to be the candle lighting up the dim corners of the busy and involved portions of our day.

The plea of not having enough time to do spiritual reading may be traceable to an inability to set priorities and to put each aspect of life in its proper perspective. If my primary commitment is the love of God, then I will take time to imbibe his word. Professional life is important, but what about all the extras that get added to it. When I look over my day, I find there is time for spiritual reading, provided I use it to its best advantage.

I may decide that I will spend fifteen minutes daily on the spiritual reading of Holy Scripture. Besides this, I may be able to set aside three one half hour periods during the week when I will do spiritual reading of other texts. This decision takes discipline and perseverance. If I only do it when I have the time, many days may go by without my doing any spiritual reading at all. On the other hand, if I have set aside time and place for this practice, I am more likely to stick to it. There may be a few days when it is not possible to follow my schedule, but these become the exception rather than the rule.

Because we have trouble quieting ourselves after other occupations, we have to be prepared to spend part of our spiritual reading time on the process of patiently slowing down our preoccupied minds so we can be as fully present to the message of God as possible. If our minds are not quieted, a hundred distractions will tug at our attention despite our best efforts to diminish them.

The conviction that we need a certain length of time to do spiritual reading is beneficial, but it should not make us scorn the five or ten minutes we sometimes find are all that we have left for God. Though we should not presume on his generosity and indulgence, we must not forget that he is capable of illuminating some bland word or trite maxim so that our spirits are transformed in a brief moment of genuine attention.

If professional life does not seem to allow us to spend as long as we need on spiritual reading, there are several questions we might want to ask ourselves. Is it really true that we cannot give more time to it or are we bestowing an exaggerated importance on certain aspects of our work?

Is what we consider a minimal amount of time really adequate to meet our spiritual needs? Compare the lot of the busy wife, who, while availing herself of daily opportunities for genuine communication with her husband, has to look forward to the weekend or the holidays to satisfy her heart's desire for a long, unhurried chat.

The intensity of professional life ebbs and flows. There are always times when we are less busy. If we can build a short time period for spiritual reading into our schedule, we will at least have our "daily bread." Then we can always give longer periods to spiritual nourishment when occasions such as a day of retreat come along.

The communication of God that comes to us in spiritual reading remains long after we have received it and makes us more sensitive to his communications in other aspects of our life.

The urge to deepen spiritual life by allowing more time for such reading can be dismissed easily in the rush of daily activities. People, problems, and plans occupy my mind, but this call, however faint and transitory, is an invitation I owe it to myself to take seriously.

To let whatever time I spend in reading become an expression of God's will for me and to experience his grace, I must be convinced that this is the place where he wants me to be at the present moment. Here his grace will exert its mysterious power, revealing to me a much more simple self beneath the surface of my anxious cares and concerns.

This period of reading acts as a bridge between daily activites and private prayer. Most of us have experienced the impossibility of moving directly from intense activities into quiet presence. We realize that spiritual reading helps to still our minds and creates an atmosphere for prayer.

Through spiritual reading I am able to discover again my inner center, often smothered amidst the noise and distractions of the everyday world. Letting myself be touched by God's words is like turning my face toward the wind and feeling its gentle force against my skin. It is like stretching out on a sandy beach and allowing the rays of the sun to penetrate my chilled body.

When I approach the word in an attitude of relaxed receptivity, it is able to spiral into the core of my being. It touches me gently and makes me aware of those areas of my life that need to be warmed by God's light. Spiritual reading helps me to see more clearly who I am before God, to realize how rich I am when I allow myself to depend solely on him.

God may use the power of the word as a means to draw me more closely to him by deepening my longings for union and communion. He may make me sense which direction he wishes me to take or how he wants me to respond.

Spiritual reading, like an encounter with a friend, is full of mystery and surprises. It is unpredictable in its demands and its revelations. Just as I cannot know in advance what to expect when meeting a friend, so I do not know beforehand how the Spirit will lead my spirit when the two come together in an encounter via the text of a holy word.

Such reading may effect me the way rest does an exhausted workman. It may bring to my tired out spirit a slow and imperceptible healing. The amount of time I devote to this practice is not as important as the attention I bring. If I am able to spend even a few minutes each day in quiet recollection and attentiveness to God's word, then undoubtedly its effects will bear lasting fruits in my life.

## IX

## *FORMATIVE SCRIPTURE READING*

\* \* \*

I would like to know more about formative scripture reading as a means of contemplating the mysteries of our faith. My tendency is to analyze scripture to the point where I neglect the mystery. Would you please comment on this aspect of spiritual reading?

\* \* \*

When geologists search for oil, it is important to locate the exact place where the "black gold" might be found. However, to locate oil is not yet to enjoy its benefits in our lives. A second phase has to be entered into: the "drilling" stage. A spiraling drill starts to bore into the exact location; it goes deeper and deeper each day and slowly but surely the hidden treasure may gush forth.

This description tells us something about our need to analyze scripture. We may try to gain precise exegetical information via the use of our ego intelligence. We should obtain that information outside the time reserved for our formative reading of scripture. Hopefully, we entrust this phase of our search to the enlightenment of Church authorities as we attempt to locate the doctrinal limits within which the revealed scripture can be safely and surely experienced, elaborated upon, and applied to our daily lives.

A spiritual or formative approach to reading scripture focuses on a prayerful, spiraling penetration of the text. Illumined by the gifts of the Holy Sprit, we dwell with the text. Our listening becomes a drilling into a delineated place and a patient waiting upon the inexhaustible treasure of the sacred word.

Spiritual reading of scripture drills for the mystery of God's presence in the crust of scriptural expression as well as in the life situations where this mystery speaks. The symbolic crust of the text always points to something more if we slow down and stay with it, letting its inner richness nourish our spirit self.

An analytical reading, by contrast, is always on the move, collecting new ideas, whereas a spiritual reading pauses repeatedly to listen to words and ideas that well up from the depths of man's life with God.

Compare what happens when we compile notes from class. We find the key ideas of the lecture, analyze its primary information, and structure the main points. But the class material will remain outside of us unless we allow it to affect us personally. Now that the key ideas are outlined, we can ask ourselves: How do I see this material verified in my attitudes or relations with others? Does this presentation ring true in my experience or in the experience of others? This stage of consideration is comparable to what happens in formative scripture reading as distinct from mere intellectual analysis.

If a group gets together for shared scripture reading, it is good to clarify what it is sharing. One member may want to bring his archeological and socio-political background while another wants to share the personal meaning a few texts had for him. Personal experience was his focus, not information.

As we listen to one another, we will find that others have experienced the same words of scripture in a different way, due to their unique temperaments and family situations, personal history and educational background. The variety of meanings each sees in scripture, the applications one makes seem endless.

Consider the phrase, "Sell all that you own and distribute the money to the poor, and you will have treasure in heaven; then come, follow me." (Lk. 18:22) For one person "all that you own" may mean time or talent; for another his possessions; for still another prejudiced attitudes that kept him closed off from others. Likewise "the poor" does not always mean the materially destitute. Are we not all poor due to original sin and the need for spiritual guidance?

To find out which meanings are appropriate to my own life, I must sit down and reflect, allow my life and the Lord's operation in it to pass before my eyes—not to analyze this mystery out of existence but to enliven its meaning.

When a friend puts a carnation on my desk, I admire its beauty and see in it a symbol of the other's caring presence. If I were a botanist, the flower would interest me both for its beauty and as a species of a floral genus.

Both ways of looking at the flower are good, but the approach is different. In the first instance I am open to its mystery and to what it says to me. I let myself be captivated by its beauty rather than taking hold of it to further my knowledge. At another time, I may need to make use of my knowledge of the flower rather than standing still to admire it.

Similarly, there are moments when I want to learn what theologians and exegetes have to say about the meaning of God's word in scripture, revealed by biblical study. Then I can bring to prayer what I have discovered in study. For example, many meanings of the story of Zaccheus may emerge from this background knowledge. Drawing upon these possibilities, I may reflect on the way in which the mercy of God is made manifest in the meeting of Jesus and the tax collector. Now I do not mull over in my mind all that scripture scholars have said about this incident; I remain quietly present to the mystery of God's mercy—no longer analyzing the scriptural passage but reflecting on it prayerfully, alone or with others. What others share with me during this time may lead me even deeper into the mystery I am reflecting upon.

Each approach—informative and formative—has its limitations and problems, but perhaps the major problem lies in mixing them up. They need not be separated but one should be in the background when the other is being used.

Just as I do not look at my flower in the same way when I admire it or study it, so I need to approach scripture with a different look at different times. The analytic look is put aside when I am involved in the look that opens me to mystery. I no longer take hold of my flower, the mystery of the scripture passage, rather I allow it to take hold of me.

In prayer and reflection, I allow God's word to speak to me through my life experiences. Quietly and peacefully, I dwell in the atmosphere of his transforming power. I recall the changes his words have effected in my life because of my personal response to scripture. I see not only its surface meanings but also the inner depths of faith made manifest in the Gospel verse.

Much of what I receive from prayer depends, of course, on my preparation, just as the "behind the scenes activity" makes for a good play. As the actors must study their lines to deliver the full intensity of the dramatist's message, so too, I must prepare myself to receive the gifts the Divine Word wishes to give me.

Scripture study helps to refine my own sensitivities to the faith horizon of the text. Because we are spirit we are always hungering for more meaning. Our thirst for God is unquenchable. We are always on the way of opening ourselves to him.

Formative scripture reading is a definite aid in our quest for God. In this exercise we are aware that a power greater than our own is at work. That power is a Person whose presence beckons us beyond what mind can contain.

The symbols and words of scripture are pointers to the Person of Jesus who wants to become one with our person. Through his words, read and meditated upon, we prepare the way for the word to enter our hearts and dwell within our being.

## X

## KEEPING A SPIRITUAL JOURNAL

\* \* \*

Could you comment on the use of the spiritual journal as a means of slowing down to develop a deeper spiritual life?

\* \* \*

"Slowing down," especially after a hectic day, allows me to savor God's gift of life. I remember, however briefly, that this day like all others was his gift. I may try to relive parts of it in memory and record my feelings and failings in a spiritual journal. Writing arouses a certain self composure and lets me slip into that peaceful readiness that awakens my spirit.

The spiritual journal itself is a means of "slowing down." First I have to take time out to do it, time away from everything else, quiet time, in solitude. This is difficult to do; the time is eaten away by many things. It takes discipline to keep that appointment with my journal, but if I do it, I will find that my writing will affect the rest of my activity.

Sometimes I seem frantic and desperate: classes, office duties, a meeting of the board of directors, follow-up telephone calls. Even though physically I may have stopped moving, my tensed muscles tell me that I am still reliving the day's round of activities.

But, I tell myself, I am busy in the service of God! In my journal I reflect on the day, on my frantic preoccupations, on how this pace is interfering with prayer. I note that praying has become only one more activity alongside others "I have to do."

If I am honest with myself, this kind of reflection will affect my spiritual life. Imagine stepping outside and taking a walk. The night air is fresh and cool. There is no traffic on the street. I am alone in stillness counting the stars. The air is delicious and I drink it in, noticing the cleansing fragrance of the trees and shrubs. My head clears. My whirling imagination calms down. I put aside the pressures and disappointments that keep my mind and emotions racing. These draughts of night air purge my feelings and give me some distance from my day.

Under the open sky, I enjoy a down to earth pleasure—the sight of stars, the smell of sweet night air. I am in touch with myself. I have the sense of being in one place and in one piece—no longer trying to sort out and keep control of dozens of factors in a daily puzzle.

I think to myself, "Today I did it again. Concentration and control. That's all I cared about. Telephone calls and office duties. Problems not people. I was not in touch with how I felt except that one moment when I tried not to lose my temper. Admit it. Only a part of me was present today—my skill and self control. Face it. This lack of involvement is what turns my activity into a treadmill."

Writing preserves these observations and enables me to return to them. In the journal I discover that my prayer life is not the integral part of my day it should be. I am Martha, busy about many things, and my spiritual life is suffering in the process. I want to slow down, but there is all that work to be done, all those people to be cared for . . . Can I be indifferent to them?

Now is the time to sit down with my journal and record this dilemma, to reflect on the directives in my life and reorder them accordingly.

Journal keeping is not a cold calculation. I place myself in God's presence. I see that I need to spend time in explicit prayer, quiet and alone. I have to slow down so that my prayer can become true prayer and my work true work—so that work "feeds" my prayer and prayer permeates my work.

The realization of the wisdom of slowing down comes with effort and practice. The spiritual journal is a means for slowing down and, at the same time, a vehicle for discovering the effect that slowing down has on my spiritual life.

Taking time to watch everyday events and recording what happens increases my awareness. For example, I drop an ice cube in hot water and am captivated by the hundreds of tiny bubbles that play along the edges of the cube, making a soft sizzling sound. All of a sudden the pressure becomes so great that the ice cube flips over on its side and disappears in the water. I think about the billions of molecules interacting with each other before my eyes and for a moment this meditation on the mystery of nature lifts me out of my ordinary life to marvel anew at the greatness of God who created the tiniest of things.

To accept the gift when it is given, to hold on to the beauty of the moment in words, is to feel refreshed in God's presence. Moments like this occur more often than we think, if we ready ourselves to notice them—as an artist or poet does.

Keeping a journal becomes a means of making me more conscious of my surroundings. In our performance oriented world we tend to live either in the past or future, fretting over what was or planning ahead. We lose touch with the present, with the shape and color of today's landscape. My journal helps me focus on the here and now.

The street, which before was merely a blur, reveals a whole way of life. I notice the expressions on the faces of the people I pass. A group of men are chatting about the ball game yesterday. A young mother tries to discipline two small children who would rather walk by themselves than take her hand. A middle-aged shopper looks regretfully at her heavy parcels.

Slowing down enables me to see the world in all its facets. Recording one message readies me to receive another. I write down in my journal memorable things that happened to me today or the reflections that are going through my mind about tomorrow. Writing enables me to see things in a new way. I become filled with wonder at the mystery of God's working in my life. I begin to sense where he is leading me from the entries in my journal. I see more clearly the way I must follow. I move toward the Center that harmonizes all sides of my experience. This sense of wholeness, of coming together with myself, is one reward of journal writing and a stepping stone on my way to God.

A friend once told me: "One of the values of the journal is to better know myself. I see it as a kind of stethoscope listening to the pulse of the self. It helps me to return to my own spontaneous response rather than the one that society expects of me. My journal also helps me discern patterns of direction. When I note repeatedly that I have chosen one path over another in a given situation—then surely this is a basic response. My journal is a means through which I come to know myself better as well as to assess my reality more objectively. It can be a tool for self understanding."

It takes conscious effort to slow down, but the result is well worth the discipline required. A good preparation for journal keeping is slowed down reading. I am not concerned about covering so much material or finishing the book; more important to me is the choice of certain passages to reflect upon during my reading time. I sit quietly to place myself in a proper mood, and then I begin to read the passage slowly. I pause when a phrase speaks to me and reflect on its meaning. I resist the urge to move on but try to stay with this meaning as long as it appeals to me.

After I have read slowly and paused to reflect, there is value in writing my reflections in a spiritual journal. Putting my comments down lets me see these words in another perspective; it helps me to appropriate their meaning.

Thomas Merton observed in his spiritual journal, *The Sign of Jonas:*

> At work—writing—I am doing a little better. I mean, I am less tied up in it, more peaceful and more detached. Taking one thing at a time and going over it slowly and patiently . . . and forgetting about the other jobs that have to take their turn.

By taking one thing at a time in patient attentiveness, I will in the end accomplish much more than by frantic running.

Once I have decided that it is necessary to slow down, I may make the mistake of trying to do so instantly. I forget that slowing down is a long process requiring time to undo bad habits. If I have been working at top speed, I cannot expect to brake instantly. The fact that I am able to say to myself, "This will take time," is a first step towards "slowing down."

Trying to quiet the rhythm of my living may result at first in fitful efforts when I am neither working well nor praying well. But I have to keep repeating to myself, "This will take time."

Being gentle in my efforts to slow down means that I respect what I am. I am not a machine with an on and off button. I have to learn to wait on myself, to become aware of my unique pace. When I notice that my hands are clenched as I sit in the bus, I relax them. When I feel that my shoulders are tensed as I hurry to classroom or chapel, I let them drop. When I catch myself rushing from one place to another, I walk more casually.

Gradually I learn to look up from my work spontaneously, to take a breath, to let my eyes go out of focus, and then to look at . . . a branch scraping against the window pane. In these moments of detachment, I become aware of God's presence in all things. I am refreshed.

A major obstacle to my efforts to slow down is the "atlas-attitude" toward life. The whole weight of the world is on my shoulders. I *must not* slacken my pace or lessen my vigilance. I *have* tremendous responsibilities.

In his *Letters from the Desert,* Carlo Carretto speaks about this sincere but deluded way of seeing things. He says:

> With this mentality I was no longer capable of taking a holiday; even during the night I felt I was "in action" . . .
> One raced continually from one project to another, from one meeting to another, from one city to another. Prayer was hurried, conversations frenzied, and one's heart in a turmoil.
>
> As everything depended on us . . . we were quite right to be worried.

It took Carretto twenty-five years to find out ". . . that nothing was burdening my shoulders . . . I had been holding up absolutely nothing. The weight of the world was all on Christ Crucified."

It may take me twenty-five years and then some to learn the same truth. To slow down is to get in touch with this mysterious gift of God that I am. Other people's standards are not my own so I don't have to strain after them. The journal I keep helps me to see that the Lord is my pacesetter. I need to stop and rest, lest I lose the serenity he allows to flow into my soul.

## XI

## SPIRIT OF POVERTY

***

Some describe poverty as an attitude toward things. Others speak of an inner spirit of detachment. What is authentic poverty? What does poverty of spirit really mean in regard to the inner life?

* * *

Such a question may make us worry about what we have and enjoy. A guilty feeling could come over us. "I have so many things for my own use while so many miss what is necessary." Instantly I begin telling myself that what matters is not that I have things but that I am detached from them. Is this attitude fully in harmony with the spirit the Lord taught us to live?

His state was divine,
yet he did not cling
to his equality with God
. . .                                                    (Ph. 2:6-7)

Christ became poor in order to enrich the lives of all people with his love and his presence. He emptied himself but God raised him high.

Temporal riches may become obstacles to spiritual wealth if we are not willing to share in Jesus' mission of service to others for love of the Father. We are not free to follow him if we are bound to our possessions in an ultimate sense.

One sign that possessions possess us is that care for them demands the major portion of our time, energy, interest and concern. Throwing away the things I have or giving them to the poor does not seem to be the whole answer—though at times and for certain people this approach may be part of the answer depending on their life situation.

There is nothing wrong with things in themselves. There is no need to feel guilty if I find myself enjoying the comforts of an affluent society. God has called us to live when and where we are. Time and energy needed to dress attractively and appropriately in relation to our world are not ill spent nor is the effort in arranging a beautiful garden or tasteful furnishings. These, too, are gifts from God and can enlarge our life and that of others. As long as they are received and enjoyed as such, poverty of spirit is possible. There is no guage that measures how much is too much, what is excessive, except our attitude. In the measure that God is the center of our life, that we are possessed by him and not by our possessions, we can experience poverty of spirit. What is luxury to one can be a normal part of life for another.

Because we are tainted by the materialism of our present society, there is no question that for a majority of us the things we own can become central at one time or another. We are literally assailed with messages encouraging acquisitiveness. Therefore, thoughts of poverty on any level seem to go against the prevailing thrust of our culture. Some say the so-called "hippie movement" grew out of the excesses of materialism; many of us, likewise, feel a need to clear our lives of the clutter of current fads and commercially whipped up needs. For some, this detachment is an important, even an essential, step toward simplicity and a God-centered life.

We should never underestimate the influence of the cultural forces around us nor the constant vigil needed to direct ourselves to Christ and away from the accepted idolatry of power and possession. Again, there is no blueprint to tell us what is too much. We need to remain on guard against being swallowed up by a surfeit of things and yet not afraid to enjoy them in the Lord in moderation and with detachment.

The attitude of poverty cannot exist in one's head divorced from any expression in the rest of life. An inner attitude must be incarnated in action if it is to be real. Christ-like presence to the Father has to embody itself concretely in day to day living. His attitude toward things must spill over in the way I possess or dispossess myself of them.

I look back over the past month. It has probably been hectic and the days ahead don't look much calmer. I grow anxious thinking about the things I have to do. How will I ever finish all of them? What if something comes up that interferes with the plans I have made? What will happen if I find more things added to the list of "must items" I already have to do?

This is certainly not the first time such concern has overtaken me, and it will probably not be the last. I begin to ask myself how an inner attitude of poverty might clean up some of the clutter clouding my mind. Perhaps a consideration of the "poverty of the present moment"—might help.

God gives me this particular day. I don't know if I will have a tomorrow, and yesterday is already gone. God gives me this particular moment. It is mine and yet I am busy worrying about the future, so preoccupied that I allow the grace of the present to pass me by. I forget about the gifts that are mine here and now and anxiously involve myself with the things of tomorrow. I forget, too, that God will give me the grace I need then to do what I have to do.

"Poverty of the present moment" is an inner attitude of treating what we have received with respect. It also influences our outer expression. Often we dream of teaching the poor, of contributing to a charitable fund; time comes and goes and we have still not realized any of these dreams because they are dreams not in tune with the present moment.

When we become aware of this moment with its limits and potentials, we may find ourselves doing what we can do realistically to help others. We awaken from our daydreams of doing big things and begin instead to appreciate the little ones we can do at this time in service of others.

When we live in respect for the present moment, we realize how rich it is. God has given us so much that we are filled to the brim. Our cup overflows and we share its contents with our brother.

What, then, is poverty in practice? Can I aspire to be "poor" while having the security of a roof over my head, food on the table, a well paying job and a place to go when I retire? I feel grateful for these benefits and do not long for any extraordinary luxuries. If poverty means being satisfied with what one "has" in a more or less detached manner, then I could indeed call myself "poor."

However, poverty of spirit includes more than an attitude of inner detachment from what one "has." It begins with a fundamental attitude of allowing God to be the center of my desires, the source of what I hope for as well as "have." The me to be satisfied becomes less central as I grow in loving surrender to him.

Once we recognize God as the source of all that is good, we can look at what we have in a new light. In authentic poverty, we realize that all we are and have is gift. We stand empty before the Father of whose fullness we all receive. Of myself I am nothing and have nothing. I have been called into existence and am sustained by an all loving God. Everything I cling to in a possessive way indicates a failure on my part to recognize that all goods are given to me.

External poverty is one means to come to inner poverty—to move Godwards. In accepting all that is ours as a gift from God, we are able to participate in Jesus' action of emptying himself so God may be glorified and others enriched.

The witness of poverty consists in giving of myself rather than of my possessions. Giving of self is more difficult that dispensing alms to the needy, for self-giving encompasses my time, talents and energies. It extends beyond an anonymous act of giving and involves me in the lives of others. There are opportunities for open giving throughout every day. Paradoxically, in giving myself to them, I may become rich.

If any thing or person stands in the way of God in my heart, I cannot become poor. I need to imitate Job's attitude in the midst of suffering and privation: "If we take happiness from God's hand, must we not take sorrow too?" (Jb. 2:10) God must be total in our lives—that is the essence of being poor. Being rid of all idols, of all extras that stand in the way of service to God and others, is the aim of spiritual poverty.

A certain fervor may prompt me to give away all but the necessities of life or at least to simplify my life and surroundings in order to come closer to God and neighbor. If this action does not spring from an infinitely more difficult inner detachment, it remains a partial gesture.

What seems to be most essential, as well as most painful, is allowing myself to be stripped of subtle attachments when these have become too central, when solicitude for persons and things supplants the attention and care I should direct to God. Only if this inner work of emptying is going on can I complement it by a certain outer simplicity.

When poverty is exercised primarily as a means to improve the fate of the poor in society, it is not Christian poverty. It is society centered instead of God centered; it has the limited nobility of humanism, but may be tainted by a subtle pride that removes us from God.

Christian poverty is ultimately a grace of God; we cannot gain this depth of inner freedom by our own powers alone. We should not only strive for poverty but more importantly pray for it as a divine gift we do not deserve.

The image of open hands seems to symbolize much of the meaning of poverty. Open hands are ready to give and receive, to be emptied and filled. They represent humility—an awareness of one's complete dependency on God, the essence of poverty of spirit.

## XII

## MORTIFICATION IN MODERN DAY
## SPIRITUAL LIFE

***

Is there a place for motification in modern life? Is the discipline of self denial needed, especially when there is so much emphasis on self fulfillment?

* * *

There are always other things we'd rather do than discipline ourselves. For instance, discipline is needed to write an answer to this question. How much more enticing it would be to watch television, read a book, entertain a friend. Many alternatives are possible. But no matter what excuses I could invent, writing should win first place. The other possibilities may be more appealing, but I have to put them aside for the present. To make this choice freely implies discipline. Surely it would be easier to turn on the TV, more relaxing to read a book or enjoyable to visit a friend, but the ministry of writing should be my main concern at this moment. It takes effort to gather my thoughts, assemble my writing materials, create an atmosphere conducive to reflection. But the reward of discipline is satisfaction for having made a commitment to the ministry God asks of me here and now.

Similar opportunities for sacrifice and discipline occur all the time. They need not be gigantic acts of denial, separated from the flow of daily life. These self-disciplines are intertwined with the life situation. Smiling kindly to someone when I have a headache, lowering the tone of my radio in consideration of a neighbor's need for quiet, learning to be punctual are some examples.

Such actions require a sensitivity that rises above personal likes and dislikes to include others' preferences. This taking into account of the other implies a sacrifice of my own concerns. Each sacrifice is an opportunity to follow Christ. The more fully I am present to the situation as his call to die and rise, the more opportunities for self denial will present themselves. My acceptance of them as a part of God's plan frees me to respond to the call of discipline and discipleship.

This positive attitude of listening goes beyond the usual negative "don'ts" associated with discipline. "Don't play in the rain." "Don't pull the apples before they are ripe." "Don't eat sweets before dinner." Don't . . . Don't . . . Don't . . . Even today as adults, we still cringe at that idea of discipline that forbade the most delicious moments of childhood—the feel of rain, the first apples, the sweet tastes.

Discipline was equated with being a "spoil sport." It was a dull affair, a tyrant. The word itself became a rod, a whip, a halt to our gallop. Added to the ordinary resistance we feel about denial is the pervasive tendency today to idolize self fulfillment. This trend is fostered by the media enticing us to rampant consumption and enjoyment of the fruits of our economy. No wonder the thought of mortification and sacrifice is distasteful.

Now we want the freedom to be fully ourselves without restraints and burdensome structures. But what does this option for freedom mean? Do I know myself well enough to become myself?

Experience teaches me something about my physical self, for example, the weight at which I feel best. I can refuse to acknowledge this truth and literally "eat myself out of shape" or I can listen to the dictates of my body and eat according to the limits of my metabolism. Do I care enough about myself to follow this truth of my organism? If I don't, what is the reason for my refusal? Is it a dislike of discipline?

Think how appalled we would be if our favorite artist, painting a fine landscape, suddenly began to daub his canvas at random because he became bored and disinterested. As regrettable is our refusal to follow the inner call to be our best selves. Lack of discipline, in this case, clearly retards our growth.

What does it mean to become a disciple? It means to follow a truth or a person who is a bearer of truth. To know myself as God's servant. To take into account what he wishes me to do in this world. To really care about myself and others.

The true disciple engages in the noblest of tasks: to unfold the masterpiece of God's creation—man himself. Discipline, far from being a stern master, is a gentle mode of love. It is that which draws the artist to complete his picture or the poet to devote himself untiringly to the word. The true disciple follows truth in loving surrender. Discipleship transcends the rough ways of willful forcing; it helps us to try again gently in spite of failure.

Daily life is replete with limiting situations that invite the attitude of discipleship. Activities are not scheduled to my liking. Lazy people ask for my help. Colleagues try me by their petty politics. I can complain about these situations or I can let them serve as reminders of human limits that prompt me to become a more responsible person. As disciple, I try to listen to the Spirit speaking in my deepest self.

Too often I am inclined to react to situations from my surface self only. This self is the result of conditioning by society I may have been trained, for example, always to respond in sweet ways to abuse and injustice. My deepest self, enlightened as it is by the Holy Spirit, may tell me to protest against abuse and injustice, even if people like me less for that and seem shocked and indignant. The best example we can find is the life of Our Lord.

His surface self, conditioned by the Jewish society of his day, would tell him to be polite when arguing with the scribes and pharisees, to keep a dignified distance from Mary Magdalene and the Samaritan woman, to ignore the businessmen in the temple instead of throwing them out and making a spectacle of himself. The Holy Spirit in his deepest self told Jesus to go against the conditioning of society in these instances, to take a stand at odds with the ways of the world at that time of history. My deepest self—enlightened by the Spirit—may sometimes inspire me to do the same, be it in less dramatic daily situations.

Rushing waters, harnessed in a reservoir, become a source of energy. Water power is available for constructive purposes. So it is, in a way, with us. We are complex beings made up of many needs, drives, emotions, and capabilities. These energies need to be channelled if they are to become opportunities for self emergence in Christ. To consider honestly who I am and what the situation calls for requires disciplined listening. I can then choose, in the light of God's design, what is the best way for me to be. This choice is made not once and for all. Rather than molding the situation statically to my liking, I listen each time to the voice of the Holy Spirit speaking in it.

Though I hear the call of Christ to live in accordance with the will of the Father, I still experience being drawn in many directions simultaneously. He asks me to act while my tired body urges me to relax. I pray that I may be more considerate of others but find myself impatient. "I fail to carry out the things I want to do, and I find myself doing the very things I hate." (Rm. 7: 15-16).

Discipline helps me to moderate these willful desires.

Through daily dying, my scattered life becomes gradually more integrated with spiritual values and convictions. Only when I make mortification an end in itself does it lose its power to transform my life in Christ.

Self denial is meant to soften and smooth the rough edges of my personality, not to turn me into an athlete of asceticism. It is meant to make me more mellow, gentle, and Christ-like. Lived wisely, mortification has a refining power, a channeling role, a capacity to set me free from the shackles of selfishness and sin.

The deepest meaning of discipleship comes into focus when I meditate upon the mysteries of Jesus' life. His death and resurrection become the pattern I must follow. Even before that paschal event, he preached the mystery of dying in order that life might flourish. He looked at the fig tree and observed that it must be pruned so new leaves could grow. (Lk. 13: 6-9) He noted that the seed dropped into the earth must die if it is to bear fruit. (Jn. 12:24) He told the young man he loved to put aside his possessions, give them to the poor, and follow him in this new way of life. (Lk. 18: 18-23)

I, too, must become aware of things in me that need to die if the Christ-life is to be born anew. The discipline of daily dying then becomes a preparation for our ultimate surrender to death.

## XIII

## *ASCETICISM AND SPIRITUAL DEVELOPMENT*

\*\*\*

What need is there for asceticism in spiritual development?
What is meant by the asceticism of the gentle life style?

\* \* \*

I am the true vine,
and my Father is the vinedresser.
Every branch in me that bears no fruit
he cuts away,
and every branch that does bear fruit he prunes
to make it bear even more.

(Jn. 15: 1-2)

These words of Christ are about the wisdom of asceticism
and its rightful place in the life of the Christian.

The ascetical dimension cannot be lived in isolation
from the invitation and inspiration of grace. The Father is
the vinedresser who prunes and trims clean. He speaks to
us as we are with our individual make-up and limitations.
He invites us gradually to strip away those things that clutter our life and stifle growth in him. Usually our *yes* to his
invitation leads us to make little acts of faithfulness in the
trying demands of daily life rather than to extraordinary
feats of self-discipline.

The Father inspires us to a gentle asceticism not only
through the events of daily life but also through our participation in the liturgical life of the Church. The various
seasons of the Church year provide a balanced rhythm of

death and resurrection, of deprivation and rejoicing. If we enter faithfully into the spirit of each season with its celebration of the divine mysteries, we will gradually find our own ascetical balance. We shall discover those things that must be trimmed away so that the Christ-life can flourish in us and yield abundant fruit.

If we neglect to take into account our unique situation within the balanced rhythm of the Church's liturgical year, we risk making ascetical practices ends in themselves. Holiness then becomes a matter of how much and how frequently we deny ourselves and inflict self punishment. We ignore the pace of grace and choose radical practices that we expect to grant us instant holiness. Such asceticism, rather than helping us to become more Christ-like, makes us barren branches, cut off their life-giving source.

This fallacy of uninspired asceticism has been repudiated in the period following Vatican II. Certain ascetical practices, several times removed from the historical, cultural, and individual context from which they had derived their meaning were seen as incompatible with today's context.

For a time the word "ascetism" itself fell into disrepute, associated as it was with anachronistic customs and excessive practices. This overreaction left a void that in turn led to a malaise in the spiritual life. Today the outlook appears more hopeful. There are signs that Christians are experiencing the need for a return to asceticism not as an end in itself but as a means of simplifying their lives so as to be more responsive to the intimations of grace.

A comparison with the art of pottery making may help us to see this need for a firm rooting of the ascetical in the soil of daily activity.

First of all, the potter chooses the clay that will have the proper plasticity and texture for the vessel he wants to shape. He kneads the moist material until all the air bubbles have been forced out of it. He then centers the ball of clay on the potter's wheel. Interestingly he does not merely throw the clay on with his hands; his whole body has to be centered, completely in balance with the wheel.

Next comes the most important phase, that of shaping the vessel, of molding the mass of clay into a cylinder by gently drawing it upward, slowly pushing on the outside while shaping from the inside. As the potter's wheel turns around and around, the fingers of the artist shape the vessel from the inside, causing it to swell at the base and narrow at the neck. This "inside work" is only possible because of the potter's steadying hand on the outside, gently working with the pressure of his fingers from the inside. Through the whole process the clay must remain moist, but not too moist; the fingers too must remain moist lest they catch on to the clay and destroy the shape of the fragile vase that begins to emerge.

The art of shaping or being shaped into our own spiritual life is similar. We cautiously need to select those few, most beneficial experiences that will give our lives the proper plasticity in tune with our unique destiny. Then the gentle asceticism of being drawn into the chosen vessel may begin. The slow, gradual push and pull of our spirituality shapes our lives from the inside as we await the work of the Master Potter who will mold us into a vessel of exquisite beauty.

As the vessel of clay is slowly shaped by being turned over and over again, so too we are gently being shaped by the daily, repetitive practices of prayer, solitude, and spiritual reading. These exercises provide the caring push and pull to direct our lives into a deeper intimacy with God. But first we must consent to the tender pressure of the Master.

St. Irenaeus aptly expresses this readiness:

It is not thou that shapest God; it is God that shapest thee. If then thou art the work of God, await the hand of the Artist who does all things in due season. Offer him thy heart soft and tractable and keep the form in which the Artist has fashioned thee. Let thy clay be moist, lest thou grow hard and lose the imprint of his fingers.

The limits we experience in daily living offer ample opportunities for asceticism. While certain acts of "doing without" may be good, the genuine acceptance of daily limitations seems to be the essential discipline of life. Extraordinary acts of self denial are often flights from the ordinary tasks of day to day dying; they carry the danger of a subtle pride. The extraordinary always includes the risk of serving our own egos in spiritual athletics in order to appear special in God's eyes.

If I am a person who is hard on myself, punishing myself rather severely for not measuring up to spiritual ideals, then I need to learn to be gentle with myself. If, by contrast, I am a person who neglects the spiritual life, then I must find the quiet everyday discipline that ties in best with ways of growing in deeper intimacy with God.

A line of the *Desiderata* reads, "Beyond a wholesome discipline, be gentle with yourself." This statement implies that we need discipline in our lives to make us gentle yet firm—to help us become the whole and holy people we were meant to be. But beyond this discipline, we need to be gentle with ourselves—understanding our limitations as human beings. God does not demand perfection of us, but only that we keep trying to love him. Can we ask more of ourselves than God asks of us? Can we seek our own perfection while not allowing ourselves to be who he wants us to be?

The gentle life allows us to see ourselves within the context of a loving God, who speaks to us words of comfort and consolation. It seems only right that the tone of voice we use towards ourselves should echo his compassion with us. This is an asceticism of the gentle life in which we become more like the loving God who calls us to share in his love with a light and joyful heart.

## XIV

## *PLAY AND THE SPIRITUAL LIFE*

\* \* \*

Please expand on the place of playfulness in the spiritual life as distinct from being deadly earnest about seeking our own perfection by not wasting a minute.

\* \* \*

A child's playfulness awakens the child in all of us and yet playfulness is often a missing ingredient in modern life. Ever since society began to equate time with money, erroneous emphasis has been placed on utilizing every minute. The playful child living in me falls into sterility. The "old man" or "old woman" begins to take over. I live as if I'm a machine or a computer.

The "job of life" is done efficiently, quickly, and completely. Life becomes a series of rigid demands. "I have to do this . . . I should do that . . . I can't waste time just being with you . . . I'm too busy getting things done."

Can the mystery and enchantment of childhood be resurrected if such is my joyless state? Playfulness depends on how freely we open ourselves to the emergence of the gentle child in each of us. Even though our world might not encourage us in this discovery, the Gospel does:

People even brought little children to him, for him to touch them; but when the disciples saw this they turned them away. But Jesus called the children to him and said, "Let the little children come to me, and do not stop them; for it is to such as these that the kingdom of God belongs. I tell you solemnly, anyone who does not welcome the kingdom of God like a little child will never enter it." (Lk. 18: 15-17)

This call to childhood does not detract from the call to labor in the vineyard of the Lord. Neither must useful activities cancel out the call to refresh and revitalize self in relaxation. The Church promotes this call in the celebration of the Lord's Day and also of numerous feasts and liturgical occasions on which work should be put aside and the people should play.

These festivities emphasize that my salvation is in God's keeping. I cannot save myself, no matter how long I work or how hard I try. Faith in God's care frees me from over concern about the results of my work. Knowing that salvation is his gift to me, I can "waste time" periodically. Refreshed by relaxation in body and spirit, I am ready to meet the difficulties of life cheerfully and playfully.

Living this balance of labor and leisure, I am able to experience the inner peace and freedom of the children of God. This point is expressed well in the following legend about John the Evangelist.

One day John was playing with a partridge, which he stroked gently with his hand. A sportsman came by and expressed his astonishment at finding him at play instead of busy at work. John said to him, "I see you carry a bow. Why isn't it strung and ready to use?" The sportsman replied, "That would not do at all. If I kept it strung it would go lax and be good for nothing." "Then," said John, "Don't be surprised at what I do."

The moral of this story is: If you insist on keeping your nose to the grindstone, sooner or later, like the taut string on the sportsman's bow, you'll either go lax and be good for nothing, or you'll snap.

It is obvious that this legend is praising play for the sake of work. As a good in its own right, play has value, but in our work-oriented society, it is difficult to be convinced of this fact. In order to appreciate it at all, or to be enticed into "wasting" some of our precious time in play, we need to look at play for the sake of work. Only when we see it as useful may we be able to tear ourselves away from some of our duties without suffering pangs of guilt. Hopefully, if we can give ourselves over to play often enough, it will eventually be experienced as a value in itself.

Play for the sake of work refers mainly to its restorative power. As a diversion from work, it relaxes us, restores our energy, and readies us to return to our tasks with renewed vigor. When we play, the child within us wins out. We close our eyes to the pile of unfinished work and take off to the mountains, the bowling lanes, the local zoo. We allow the spirit of play to take over. The solemn call of duty fades into the distance and we feel carefree. We let our guard down and delight in the present moment.

Not only do we return from play with a renewed energy and outlook; we often return with new insights in the work we were grappling with before. While at play, unfinished plans and scattered pieces of information had time to incubate within our minds; sometimes they mesh like so many pieces of a jig-saw puzzle.

Once we experience how play enhances work, we may also discover some positive changes in our life as a whole. We may not be so tense and anxious as before—so prone to be impatient with ourselves and others. We may learn to drop the deadly serious attitude toward life where I am the sole doer. Even our prayer life becomes more relaxed. Play makes it easier to give ourselves over to God's care and to let him play with us.

What is work for one person may be play for another. For a symphonic artist music is serious business; for an amateur guitar player it is simply fun. As he takes his guitar out of its case, he lets subside his preoccupation with the work piled on his desk and begins to strum his favorite tune. He switches from chord to chord playfully in no set pattern, creating his own rhythmical expression. As he plays, he seems to be expressing his own feelings, moods, and thoughts of the day. His whole self is caught up in the music. Time stands still. The thirty minute session seems to be over in five.

Our task oriented society may label play a waste of time, but it frees a part of my personality that lies deeper than my ability to accomplish the tasks at hand. Play is a time break in the life of service and obligation. It gathers my whole self together and is comparable to what happens when I pray. It helps me to realize that I do not always have to be an achiever in life; I can also be a celebrator of what is given. By making room for play in my schedule of duties, I follow the way of wisdom who was by God's side, a master craftsman, delighting him day after day, "ever at play in his presence,/at play everywhere in his world,/delighting to be with the sons of men." (Pv. 8: 30-31)

There is no playfulness possible when we feel weighed down with worry and refuse to waste a minute. What can be more flitting than a flock of sparrows pecking bread crumbs yet our Father in heaven makes their care his personal concern. (Mt. 6: 25-34) Instead of filling every minute, it might be good to take time off and enjoy all that is.

Play will only gain in this freedom as long as it remains truly play. Our achievement orientation may be so strong that we turn every play into a feat of grim performance. Anxious competition may take over and make relaxation impossible. The tennis ranch may become another place of work where we must compulsively prove our worth. Mountain travel may deteriorate into a struggle against time and fellow travellers, an endurance test that blinds us to the breathtaking vistas all around. If we lose our capacity for play, we also lose our capacity for contemplation, for "useless" presence to the Divine.

Will the earth cease to spin on its axis if we take an hour or two to let the breeze blow through our hair? In that moment of playful surrender, we might experience the Lord at play in the world. We let all control and rigidity flow out of our system and float toward the Father who is waiting for us. His presence buoys us up. He urges us to cast our cares upon him, to let go of our burdens and to trust as children do, that the Father who created us cares for us always.

## XV

## *FREEDOM AND OBEDIENCE*

\* \* \*

Please reflect on the desire for personal freedom in the context of obedience.

\* \* \*

Human freedom does not mean doing what I want to do when I want to do it, for human freedom is always limited and situated. On the side of *freedom,* we are open to new possibilities. We can choose the direction our life will assume. On the side of *limits,* this ability to choose is determined by many factors: age, background, biological and psychological make-up, education and choices made up to the present moment.

A girl born and raised in South America, for instance, is not likely to become a congress woman in the United States. A man who has chosen to marry cannot live a bachelor life. We are all bound by some limits. Openness to God in the midst of these human limits is the meaning of religious obedience. It is a way of listening to the spiritual potential of our life within the bonds of natural and cultural limitedness.

Negative views of obedience emerge in an ego-oriented culture that stresses independence of action and reliance on personal insight and ambition. We may find in ourselves the tendency to want things our way and to see as God's will only those areas of apostolic endeavor that seem most essential to us.

Religious obedience widens our perspective. It orients our choice toward whatever truly serves a fuller spiritual life. Through religious obedience we listen to reality; we perceive our surroundings with clarity. We are less likely to cut ourselves off from those things that may be an expression of God's will even if they do not tie in with what we judge to be our life direction.

Personal freedom and religious obedience complement one another. We need both aspects to temper that ego-centeredness that could easily distort the situation. In responding to people, events and things, we must take a stand. Here personal freedom is apparent. By making a choice, by taking on the responsibility it entails, we grow. If we just float along wherever life leads, we may never grow to be the unique person God is calling us to become.

To become fully human, we must remain open to reality, to what is really there. By ourselves we are able to perceive only a limited view. By listening to what others have to say, we can check our perspective as well as broaden it through their experience. This wider view in turn calls forth a better, though still limited, response. Because we are free, we are able to respond personally to each situation, to discern its meaning for our life here and now. Thus obedience and freedom are complementary guides to mature personal growth.

It is always tempting to think of freedom as having no limits until we take a realistic view of daily living. For example, if I am tone deaf my condition immediately limits my freedom to choose a career as a pianist. If I feel nauseous in the presence of people who are sick, my freedom to become a good nurse is severely curtailed. My secure or shaky financial situation tells me if I can purchase the car I see in the showroom or the one in the used lot.

Everyday experience reveals again and again how limited

I am as a human being. Everytime I opt for a specific direction, I add even more limits to this freedom, though, of course, choice also opens new possibilities. I choose to place certain restrictions on one area of my life for the purpose of intensifying life in another area. For example, if I choose to join a religious community, I give up many aspects of life in the world for the sake of developing a life style that may help me to deepen my union with God. At the same time I open myself to centuries of experience of people who are experts in the basic ways of spiritual living. Though I sacrifice a part of my personal freedom, I gain the possibility of living within a framework approved by the Church and demonstrating a distinct facility in the common ways that concretize the spiritual life.

A friend was teaching elementary school in a little town in upstate Pennsylvania in spite of the fact that she eagerly wished to be at the University finishing her degree in home economics. She neither liked being in a place with so little cultural stimulation nor did she enjoy the other teachers she met there. How could she live happily in such a situation when her heart longed to be elsewhere?

Until now she had simply tolerated the situation. On the surface, she presented a facade of pleasantness but interiorly she felt bitter and negative. "I do not want to be here at all but I need the money . . ." She felt constrained by her circumstances and could not see beyond the misery she experienced. But could there not be another response to this same scene?

Yes, she acknowledges her dislike for teaching there. She neither denies this experience nor fixates on it. Rather she turns it into a means of growth. She realizes how disappointed she is that her dream of getting the degree will have to be postponed. She accepts the discouragement of working with people who do not share her outlook or empathize with her need. Now she chooses to accept disappointment rather than merely tolerating her position and feeling negative toward it. She willingly yields to the whole situation with its limitations and makes the best of it. She lets all the disadvantages subside and addresses herself to the positive features.

This free response of refocusing lessens her resentment. She becomes more present to the task at hand and decides that one year more or less won't interfere with her degree. This second response illustrates the fact that freedom means choosing to accept the limited reality of the situation in which I find myself. No situation is perfect. I must take a stand toward my circumstances and develop the proper positive response that signals true maturity.

Look at Jesus whose food and drink was to do the Father's will. In the Garden of Gethsemane, he was faced with death. What fear and discouragement must have flooded his being. Yet he freely responded to the Father: ". . . if you are willing, take this cup away from me. Nevertheless, let your will be done, not mine." (Lk. 22: 42-43)

In our experience of living obedience in freedom, we are bound to meet situations in which, like Jesus, we are asked to do things that do not seem agreeable from our point of view. Despite this response, we can choose to accept the situation and search for the possibilities it holds. Moreover, we can place our choice in the wider perspective of Christ's acceptance of his Father's will even unto death.

A delicate sense of hearing is required to catch that perfect pitch of God's voice in such imperfect situations. Can we dare to hope that our ears will be so delicately attuned to the voice of God? Can we be so stilled in our desires that we desire in purity of heart only to obey his will?

To listen with my mind already made up is an empty gesture. Only when I allow the voice of God to release my inner freedom from the bonds of pride and willfulness that enslave me, can I discover the purpose for which I alone was made.

## XVI

## SPIRITUALITY AND ADDICTION TO EMOTION

\* \* \*

Various articles refer to an addiction to excitement, emotionalism, and sensationalism in spirituality. What is the correct relation between spirituality and our emotional expressions?

\* \* \*

The word "addiction" means to give up or over. The drug addict likes the feeling of being high because he no longer has to face the responsibilities and burdens of being an ordinary human being. He gives himself over to his addiction in an attitude of impotent passivity as opposed to a healthy and alive receptivity.

Addictive existence is thus a giving up of one's possibility to stand out in the world. It is usually accompanied by a pervading sense of brokenness within the self. The addicted person can no longer stand up without the help of some physical or emotional crutch. The real self God calls forth in him, however talented or limited, is not acceptable, so he overlays that self with an unreal self, artificially stimulated or inflated. Because he cannot cope with his own uniqueness nor with the otherness of the world, he attempts to fuse with reality. He begins to lead a parasitic kind of life, grafting himself onto the exciting, the stimulating, the sensational.

Negative influences in his personal history make him passively retreat from the world of ordinary responsibilities. To go back to the womb and start all over again is impossible, but he still seeks womb or maternal substitutes by sucking on a weed, swallowing a pill, surrendering blindly to a cause, fusing with another person in a counterfeit love, or seeking religious exaltation as an opium of escape.

This stimulating experience is used to escape the day to day commitments, duties and challenges of life. The person becomes passively dependent on the sources of stimulation and opposed to anyone who questions him or tries to remove him from them.

What relation is there between such addictive expressions of emotion and spirituality? True spirituality implies basic principles, conditions, and structures while spirituality-as-escape has connotations of lack of structure, excitement, and feelings that are out of control. However, just as on a sailboat, the rudder and the sails work together to guide the boat on its course, so too it is possible to respect and live one's emotions and to live spiritually as a unified whole.

The rudder on the boat is the vertical blade at the stern of the vessel used for directing, guiding and keeping the boat on its course. The position of the rudder will direct the boat to head into the wind, moving with it or against it. This position determines if the sails will catch the wind, billow out and cause the boat to glide over the water. Without the guiding direction from the rudder, the sails flap and wave uselessly in the wind, tossing the boat to and fro as it drifts aimlessly along, with the danger that the sails will either be torn by the wind or cause the boat to capsize.

Spirituality is analogous to the function of the rudder on a sailboat. It gives us guidelines and directives for the daily living of God's will as well as greater insight into the basic dynamics of spiritual life. It helps us to discover and stay on the way.

Emotions are like the sails of the boat, affected by the wind, responding to the spirit of the times or to the Holy Spirit blowing where he wills. Our sails must be guided and directed by the rudder, that is, emotions must be guided by spirituality if we are to keep on our course towards intimacy and union with the Divine.

If our emotions are allowed to run loose, flapping aimlessly and waving in the breeze, seeking only their fulfillment rather than being at the service of a greater task, then the result may be mere emotionalism, which, as Kahil Gibran says in *The Prophet,* ". . . if unattended, is a flame that burns to its own destruction." Instead of enriching spirituality through more vibrant participation, emotion detracts us from our original destination. The sails become more important than the boat needed to complete our journey.

Just as excessive dependence on alcohol is damaging to a person's health, emotionalism—excessive dependence on emotions—is detrimental to one's spiritual life. Whether I smoke three packs of cigarettes a day or watch soap operas all afternoon, whatever I do in excess, I will more likely than not find many good reasons for it. Others' excesses are always much easier to identify than my own. These I rationalize away. I try to convince myself that it is better to smoke than to be crabby all the time; that afternoon serials are not so "far-fetched" and that "you'd be surprised at the number of intelligent people who watch them." So it is difficult to see my own excesses as excesses.

We may identify as an "addict to emotionalism" only the person who demands highly emotional experiences in prayer. He may not attend Mass unless there is soothing guitar music, shared homilies, and physical demonstrations of affection. He may find liturgy dull and uninspiring when it fails to evoke a state of bliss. Such an attitude seems to equate liturgy with an emotional "high" and is, therefore, unrealistic—removed from the true essence of worship.

Emotionalism can take another form. Holding tenaciously to the traditional, regardless of what authoritative directives have taught to the contrary, is as much an example of emotionalism as the search for something sensational.

What these two forms of emotionalism have in common is a missing rational component. Refusing to consider the validity of any view but my own always implies an excessively emotional stance, regardless of how unemotional I may appear.

The fact that I do not identify myself with the "excitement addicts" does not mean that I am not as prone to emotionalism. Whatever I cling to in an unthinking way is what makes me excessively emotional. It may be an exclusive attachment to the singing of Gregorian chant or an unwavering demand for country music at Mass. In each situation, I am acting out of excessive emotion.

Religious feelings belong to the most sacred moments of man's experience. Unfortunately, his search for the sublime is misdirected by feelings that have become excessive.

I cannot turn off my emotions in the way I can the radio or television. I may try to calm the angry feelings I experience or the upsurge of excitement at good news, but I find that these emotions are with me just the same. The angry feelings evoked by an experience that happened a short time ago still color my interaction with others and often prevent my listening to the whole situation.

When I become emotionally involved in prayer or liturgy, I may find myself becoming increasingly addicted to the "golden glow" I experience. Warm feelings may become the only trustworthy indications in my mind that my prayer is going well. I can become so reliant on these feelings that I lose sight of other realities of the spiritual life, such as aridity and the need for faith, obedience and the perseverance it implies. This preoccupation with self makes me focus on my experience instead of on the Lord.

I forget that in searching for the emotional excitement of thunder and fire, I may fail to hear God in the "gentle breeze." (1 K. 19:13) Emotions do have a place in my approach to God, but if they become dominant, they can hold my attention so much that prayer becomes a listening to self rather than a self giving to the Lord.

This is not to say that religion should revert to being a matter of do's and don'ts rather than a personal faith relationship with God. God is our loving Father and we are his children. This simple truth of doctrine is meant to touch not only the intellect but also the heart.

The words of the psalmist describe this harmonious approach well:

> God, you are my God, I am seeking you,
> my soul is thirsting for you,
> my flesh is longing for you,
> a land parched, weary and waterless;
> I long to gaze on you in the Sanctuary,
> and to see your power and glory.
>
> (Ps. 63: 1-2)

These words manifest a living faith made concrete in liturgical experience and communal participation.

Genuine spiritual living always requires balance. Without doctrinal knowledge, religious experience risks becoming mere emotionalism; without religious experience, doctrinal knowledge tends to remain abstract and divorced from life.

Christ commands us to love God not with our mind or with our heart, but rather with all our heart, all our soul, all our strength and all our mind. (Lk. 10:27) Authentic spiritual living involves, therefore, our whole self in a loving relationship of faith in a God we dare to call Our Father.

## XVII

## *SPIRITUAL LISTLESSNESS*

\* \* \*

What can we do when a kind of spiritual listlessness takes over making prayer, meditative reading, and reflection on the words of scripture difficult, if not impossible. Are there any practical suggestions for overcoming the problem of listlessness which acts as an obstacle to concentration on and dwelling with the word?

\* \* \*

How foolish I felt after picking up my wallet and car keys, walking to the car on my way to attend a meeting, driving along, and suddenly becoming aware that instead of going to the meeting I had automatically driven the route I take each morning to school. The mechanical action of following my usual morning route, completely oblivious of where I should have been going, makes me wonder how this error could have happened.

I recall how "out of it" I had been at dinner, sitting there like a spectator. Other factors hit me. During a recent telephone conversation, a friend had commented on how distant I sounded.

Reflection on this experience helps me to see what happens in general when listlessness takes over. In this case I came to the awareness of my loss of spirit from performing an action automatically and finding myself on the wrong road. I felt forced to reflect on my relationships with others and with God. I discover a similar pattern in both cases. Dryness in prayer is comparable to the emptiness felt in my routine engagements.

Aware of the problem, I can now consider what is blocking the depth of my relationships with others and my intimacy with the Lord. I seem the victim of "too much" and "too many" projects and concerns. As a result I am lacking in relaxed presence to the here and now. A realization of my limits is needed in order to admit that I cannot do it all, that I have to let go of some projects to provide room for the Lord to dwell within me.

Some of us tend to increase our involvements and the longer we cling to them, the more we insist they are necessary. If we were to sit quietly and enumerate every activity of our day, then generally of our week, all the while gaining a little distance from our routine, inevitably we would discover the non-essentials. Then we must gently remove them in order to create a rhythm in our lives, leaving space for the serenity that is part of prayerful presence.

An important prerequisite for this refocusing is listening to our body, getting in touch with its messages. When are we most tired or most alert? Where can we go to rest in God with the least distractions? When is the best time and place for prayer?

Reflection upon the obstacles to our spiritual life may lead to a change of direction, but this must be done in a patient, practical and loving manner, expecting no instant cure.

We must learn to listen to listlessness and fatigue and to bring them to prayer for God's healing. We come to God's presence with a recognition of where we are and proceed from there. Sometimes that may mean a mere reading of the word rather than reflection on it. Or, due to fatigue, we may be able only to manage a simple repetition of a single meaningful phrase.

If listlessness and fatigue persist, we must seek remedies. These tend to be individual and vary with the intensity of one's disposition. We must first take a look at the causes of our lassitude. Are we trying to fit prayer time into the free moments that might happen along, or are we maintaining a disciplined perseverance? Are we seeking to keep God central in our lives or have we given that place to some project or person who continually gains our attention during times of prayer? Do we seek God's presence or do we come to prayer and spiritual reading as one of many duties to be taken care of formally? Are we patient or do we demand an instant effect of prayer?

Such reflections enable us to identify with St. Paul's urgency to keep alert in prayer, never give up, and follow the lead of the Spirit. (Col. 4:2; Eph. 6: 18-20)

We have to want to be in God's presence in order to listen to his Word. We have to desire this word deeply enough to lift ourselves out of our listlessness, distractions, and subtle self pity—to come before him just as we are at the moment. Then the words of scripture hold life and meaning: "When you seek me you shall find me, when you seek me with all your heart; I will let you find me (—it is Yahweh who speaks . . .) (Jer. 29:13-14)

St. Therese of Lisieux has written:

> Do not believe I am swimming in consolations; oh, no, my consolation is to have none on earth. Without showing Himself, without making His voice heard, Jesus teaches me in secret; it is not by means of books, for I do not understand what I am reading. Sometimes a word comes to console me, such as this one which I received at the end of prayer . . .

Clearly listlessness, fatigue, boredom, distaste, aridity are all familiar companions on the spiritual journey; even the saints had to endure them. There are many times when the spirit is willing but the body is weak and lethargic or the spirit seems weighed down with lassitude, and this state may last for a long time.

The fathers of the desert called such spiritual fatigue "acedia." Their advice was to stay in the cell and stick it out. They knew that acedia, if it was sent by God as a purification, would only disappear when it had done its work. They were not afraid of this sense of emptiness, this desert experience because they believed that the Lord leads us into the desert in order to speak to our heart. (Ho. 2:14)

It is wise to remember that commitment of the will to the glory of God is more important than surface feelings of listlessness. We have to maintain a simple attentiveness to God in spite of the way we feel. God does not ask us to be wide awake and full of inspiration every time we pray; he asks us to pray no matter how we feel. Love of God, worship in spirit and truth, are possible in the desert; they gain in purity.

Fatigue reminds us of our humanness and teaches us that God is the master of all experience. Accepting our limits allows us to turn to Jesus in the Gospel. We reflect on how he responded to others and to his situation when tired. We watch him at the well with the Samaritan woman. Though he is exhausted he speaks kindly to her and offers her the waters of everlasting life. We see him playing with the children or boating with friends after long days of teaching. He knows from experience what it means to feel tired and will help us to alleviate it—if we cooperate by trying to discover the cause of excessive fatigue.

Perhaps we are worried or anxious about our tasks or problems. Maybe we are working too hard for our own physical and mental well being. Are we eating properly and getting enough rest? Sometimes there are several reasons for our listlessness and there are times we cannot find any one cause. We must look for ways to come out of these periods while learning to accept them.

We may need additional rest and relaxation in order to facilitate our dwelling with the word. Perhaps we can seek another time for prayer and reflection—more conducive to our present low level of energy. Most of all we have to accept the fatigue as part of us. We cannot ignore it, just as we would not ignore a broken arm or a sluggish heart beat. Hence, we must remain gently faithful to spiritual reading, reflection and prayer, while waiting as patiently as possible for the healing recovery from listlessness that allows for concentration and openness.

When we can do nothing else, we may offer God the "prayer of fatigue." We can say to him: "Here I am, Lord, weary and listless and drained as usual. I have nothing to offer but a worn out body and a tired spirit. But what I have and what I am, I offer to you, O Lord, with all my heart."

God accepts the way we feel, so why can't we? God loves the weary I as much as he loves the wakeful. Our love for him runs far deeper than our state of weariness, even though that weariness seems to have penetrated every corner of our being.

It is comforting to know that God will not turn away from us because of our listlessness and fatigue. In fact the Gospel tells us that Jesus extended a special invitation to weary souls when he said: "Come to me, all you who labor and are overburdened, and I will give you rest." (Mt. 11: 28)

## XVIII

## LONELINESS AND SPIRITUAL GROWTH

* * *

Many people feel alone and lonely. Is loneliness an obstacle to spiritual growth or can it be an aid in disguise?

* * *

To answer this question, we need to make a distinction between two kinds of loneliness that influence each other. Primary loneliness is being cut off from God. As long as we live our lives without him, investing all our energies elsewhere we will eventually experience the disappointments of a superficial existence. We will have severed ourselves from the only abiding comfort there is—union with God. When God is first in our lives and encompasses us totally, there is no room for loneliness. We are filled by the Divine.

People who held an unquestioning belief in God, like the early and medieval Christians, were not only supported by their faith, but it linked them firmly to all of God's creation. They lived out their lives in a simple faith in God's presence and providence. There was less room for loneliness.

As insights from science and technology slowly eroded man's consciousness of his connection to God, we suffered a sense of alienation. As we cut ourselves off from our Divine Source, an anxious loneliness filtered into our lives. The further we ventured from God, the deeper our loneliness and subsequent despair became.

Each of us is affected by this obstacle of alienation, for

even the most devout Christian is part of his society and cannot escape the prevailing implications of scientism and humanism. It is our lifelong call as Christians to discover and rediscover in faith our certitude of God's presence in creation and of his intimate nearness to us. Whenever we let loose of this divine thread, we will experience the malaise of our time—loneliness.

As man turned away from God, his need for others increased. In order to counter his vague uneasiness, he surrounded himself with activity—with people, noise, competitive projects—with anything that would distract him from his gnawing sense of incompleteness. He made his working, achieving, social dimension the ultimate value in life, neglecting his elusive spiritual self. None of us can operate in today's world without being influenced in some way by this thrust.

And yet we know from experience that frenzied togetherness only moves us further from our source. We need times alone, in solitude, to help us see our way through the maze of conflicts and ambiguities in which we live. Being alone cannot be equated with loneliness, unless we have forfeited our connection to God.

Secondary loneliness comes from withdrawal from our neighbor, associates, family. It happens when we wall ourselves off from authentic encounter. Such encounter is never a matter of infantile fusion but of being with others while respecting our mutual uniqueness. Sometimes withdrawing from people is a reaction to the draining aspect of togetherness or the meaningless din of activity that surrounds us. Whatever the cause, secondary loneliness is a form of isolation which turns us in upon ourselves. It, too, is a denial of God and of others.

In primary loneliness we disobey the first part of the great commandment—to love the Lord our God with our whole heart and soul and mind. In secondary loneliness we violate the command which follows—to love our neighbor as ourselves.

Basically, then, loneliness is a matter of disobeying or of not listening, of not caring enough to care about others. It is an introspectionistic movement. We become filled with the minutia of our own existence. We cannot make the generous gesture to reach beyond our self preoccupation to someone else.

There are countless opportunities to get out of one's self, to touch and be touched by another. There are the disheartened to cheer, the sick to visit, the frustrated to calm. There is always someone who needs our ear, our compassion. It is impossible to feel lonely when we are doing something for someone else, when we go the extra mile.

We can, for instance, take the initiative to be the hostess of a family evening or help someone else prepare a surprise for the group. These moments of caring pull us away from feeling sorry for ourselves or feeling left out. Being present to others, complimenting them on their ways of being thoughtful, trying to stop and listen to their cares—such outgoing acts as these help us to look beyond our lonely world.

As long as we remain in the prison of our loneliness, we cannot grow in the dimensions of real love, which find their roots in God. If we begin to reach out to others, they will reach out to us. We shall be like the virtuous woman in Proverbs:

> She gets up while it is still dark
>   giving her household their food,
> . . .
> She holds out her hand to the poor,
>   she opens her arms to the needy.
> . . .
> She is clothed in strength and dignity,
>   she can laugh at the days to come.

(Pv. 31: 15-25)

## XIX

## FAITH AND FEAR OF DEATH

\* \* \*

I am experiencing a deep fear of death. Is this a sign of lack of faith in God?

\* \* \*

Fear of death is part of being alive. There is in each of us an innate drive to live forever. Faith in God helps us to cope with our fear of death. Enlightened by the grace of the Holy Spirit, we can submit our fears to the redeeming love of God, who lets us see death, in Jesus, not as an end, but as a new beginning.

We feel little certitude about the most certain event in life, death. Faith in Jesus' promise of life eternal gives us the certitude we need to look upon death as the transition to a fuller life.

The thought of death is the Lord's way of calling us beyond ourselves. Faith in him gives us wings to reach beyond this life with a joy born of hope. In one sense fear of death has nothing to do with faith in God. It is part of my nature. In another sense, faith in God has everything to do with fear of death. It gives meaning to the high point of life.

I can imagine myself sitting in the back seat of a car with my eyes closed and my fists clenched, praying as hard as I can because my driver is speeding on a rainy road. I keep my eyes shut. I cannot sit still, much less concentrate on prayer. Suddenly I open my eyes and see that I am slanting straight toward a ditch. The car is out of control. I scream, go limp, and then it's over. In the space of a few seconds the car is lifted up, turned on its side, and thrust into a ditch. There was no screeching or thudding, not even a jostling bump.

The driver, my companions and I crawl out of the top of the car without a scratch. Still I feel the panic of that moment, the cold sweat, the shortness of breath. I was sure that this was it, and I was terrified. Why? Was it the fear of death or of dying? Of being mangled and torn apart? Of the suffering such a violent death might inflict? Was it dread of meeting the Lord on the other side while not being ready for him? Was it the fear for others, for my family dependent on my care?

All of these fears were probably present, at least implicitly, but first and foremost is the normal human desire to cling to life as our most precious possession. All of us hang on to the gift of life when it is threatened. Only by an act of surrender are we able to relinquish our hold on it.

Looked at from a merely human perspective, death is a separation from all we hold dear, or it is seen as a release from the misery brought about by old age, sickness or poverty. In spite of all our complaints and anxieties, most of us would prefer to suffer our present ills than to launch out into what we do not know—that dimension of life from which no telecasts have been beamed back.

Faith in God overcomes this fear and opens up a whole new vista for us. As we learn to see ourselves as the finite creatures we are, we trust our Creator to bring us to fulfillment. As we say *yes* to his shepherding of our lives, we realize that we are not in ultimate control. We are then more able to relax and face the moment he calls us from one form of life to another. To the faithful person death is not an undesirable end but a welcome passageway to life eternal.

Fear can either inhibit my freedom or elicit awareness of

my dependence on God as the basis of true freedom. Fear of death may be a call to withdrawal or to conversion and radical recommitment. It does not necessarily bespeak a lack of faith; rather it gives me an opportunity to know myself in relation to the gift of life given to me by God.

Life is a gift given in order to be surrendered. Daily we live through sickness, pain, loneliness, disappointment—little deaths that make us aware of how little control we have over our lives. We fear letting go until we really listen to the words of Jesus:

> Anyone who loves his life loses it; anyone who hates his life in this world will keep it for the eternal life. Jn. 12:25

Then we know that it is only in surrender of our life to painful uncertainties that we can possess it.

Since we only pass once from death to eternal life, we never get the opportunity to become familiar with it. Death is a topic shunned in most conversations, yet it remains in our thoughts more often than we mortals care to admit. What makes death so terrible that the thought of it causes us to be afraid? One reason seems to be letting go of the familiar.

Does this mean that God, who is our loving Father, can no longer be seen as One in whom we can place our faith and trust? This distrust could happen if we give in to our fears and allow them to take hold of us.

Faith in God is a free gift that we must use in order to possess it more fully. Mary led a life of faith and one can plainly see how much pain and suffering she endured, but each new crisis seemed to make her a woman of stronger faith.

We can see what has gone by in the past and accept this suffering as a basis to grow in faith, but the future has not yet been revealed to us. Faith is a virtue, not an emotion;

that is why we may mistake our fears and anxieties for a lack of faith. We must practice our faith and trust in God as we face the unknown and unfamiliar. Our faith will then sustain us, even when we feel as if it is no longer present.

In the face of suffering and death, Christ himself shed drops of blood and besought his Father to "take this cup away from me." (Lk.22:42) Fear of death can thus be seen as a sign of faith rather than as a weakness, provided we attend to the warning: "You too must stand ready, because the Son of Man is coming at an hour you do not expect." (Lk. 12:40)

Consciously or unconsciously, the human mind can never fully free itself from its final scene. But to say that fear of death is a sign of weakness would be to make cowards out of the bravest men and women in history. Just as it is true to say that "The fear of Yahweh is the beginning of knowledge," (Pv. 1:7) so a salutary fear of death is a sign of wisdom as well.

The fear of death seems to decrease as the strength of faith increases. Still the fear is inherent because we are not created to die but to live. Human nature recoils from death. Every instinct in our bodies turns toward life. Our entire physiology is geared for the struggle. The separation of soul and body is an unnatural phenomenon and no man can free himself from the dread of this parting. It is a leap in the dark from which there is no return. Only faith tells us it is a leap into the waiting arms of Our Lord.

Christ has prepared a place for us in his Father's house and we must focus our attention on this promise in order to allay our deepest natural fears. In Jesus alone can the fear of death go hand in hand with a deep act of faith.

## *XX*

## *AGING AND THE DARK NIGHT OF FAITH*

\* \* \*

The dark night that seems endless often comes when one is middle-aged and already experiencing stress in life. What helps me to remain faithful when I feel like giving up?

\* \* \*

As we move into winter, it is obvious that nature has changed her scene. Autumn has stripped the trees and their colorful foliage is a thing of the past. The change of seasons is an integral part of nature's year. Although we often wish to hasten the dismal winter days toward spring, we realize that one season is needed to bring about the other. So we wait patiently.

Human nature affords us the same possibility of changing seasons that seem to be interwoven in our life cycle. In the "summers" of life, we experience exhilaration, openness, the freedom to challenge and be challenged. In "autumns" we suffer a loss or a stripping of vitality. In the "springs" we know the wholeness and growth of peace and joy. Before this time of newness and growth, there was "winter"—a period of defeat, or a time of struggle and suffering.

To most of us, winter seems bleak and dead while in actuality growth is taking place in hiddenness, below the soil. During the winter months, plant life withdraws to recoup its forces and to prepare for the new thrust of spring.

With adequate reflection, we may see the same cycle of nature exemplified in our own lives. There are stages throughout life when we must withdraw into our inner center and let the darkness come upon us. During middle age life seems to lose its meaning and obligations become oppressive. At this time weariness often takes over.

As we do not see what is happening below the surface during nature's winter months, so in faith we must believe that although he is presently unseen, God is affecting an interior growth in us. Being at home with this mystery may help us to wait patiently and live through the darkness.

If we believe that this darkness is from God, we may find that he is calling us to a deeper commitment: to shed the darkness of what we feel for the light of who we are.

In our solitude we may discover that we are extinguishing the light ourselves by our overly active life, by our "doing" in preference to our "being," by interior noise rather than quiet. If we honestly evaluate ourselves in this season of our life, we may see that the darkness is in reality a light to see what must be changed. Then in God's time he may once again bring forth within us a new spring and a realization that

> . . . winter is past,
> the rains are over and gone.
> The flowers appear on the earth.
> The season of glad songs has come,
> the cooing of the turtledove is heard
> in our land.

> (Sg. 2: 11-12)

As we seek to open ourselves to ever deeper experiences of God's presence, we may have to endure prolonged periods when we feel abandoned by the One who promised to be with us always. In the past we may have felt joy and sensible peace when we prayed; this experience of God's presence seemed to permeate our whole life. We knew that God was always with us, that he truly was our rock of refuge, our loving Father. We felt as secure and content as the child who slips his hand into his mother's. God knew that our faith was not yet strong enough to bear the painful lack of consolation.

Now when we try to pray, there are no "good feelings." We feel as if God has withdrawn from us and is far away. This is the time when we need "pure faith"—the kind of faith that believes in God's constant loving presence, even when there is no consolation, no sensible sign of his nearness.

Spiritual masters like St. John of the Cross assure us that through such a "dark night of the soul" God is preparing us to experience deeper, more contemplative forms of prayer. In fact the dark night seems to be a necessary period of purification for a more mature relationship with God, just as the endurance of physical separation from his mother prepares the child for a more mature relationship with her.

Our loving Father is asking us to trust him even in darkness and lack of consolation. He is asking us to identify with his Son on the cross, who in his dark night of suffering prayed: *"My God, my God, why have you deserted me?"* (Mt. 27:47). If we can pray these words with faith then God may also help us to gently surrender ourselves to him as Jesus did while praying: "Father, *into your hands I commit my spirit."* (Lk. 23:46)

In faith we believe that the God who raised Jesus from the dead, will also raise us from our death-like dark night and bring us into the light of resurrection. In this light we are illumined and transformed in God, as St. John of the Cross explains in poetic affirmation:

O night that has united
The Lover with His beloved,
Transforming the beloved in her
   Lover.

The fact of not being able to see and to control the situation is at the heart of every dark night experience. We do not choose it. It falls upon us, with all its heaviness, its meaninglessness, its boredom. We do not see any more; we do not know any more. We are no longer in control of the situation. We do have a choice either to let go in faith, or to become more and more frustrated. In a dark night experience there is no way out. There is only a way through and that is the way of letting go.

We find it hard to let go; we fight a great deal in order to defend our possessions; we refuse to be stripped of our holdings and left alone in the nakedness of our small and limited beings.

If we respond in trust and faith to these experiences, even though painful, we will be able to sing with St. John:

> O guiding night!
> O night more lovely than the dawn!

The Father in his tender love gives us an opportunity to face our human condition, and to discover on a level of deep intimacy the mercifulness of his love.

As we grow in wisdom and age before God and men, we also grow in the awareness of our own limitations. We no longer have illusions of unlimited strength, endurance, potential. Our world becomes smaller, but it also becomes more real. Ideally speaking, we have a better awareness of who we are and what we can do. Especially in the beginning phase, this awareness can be painful. We feel a dull emptiness in the face of all the things we are not and all the things we have not done.

Such is the crisis of middle-age. Faced with this crisis I have to make a choice: either to dwell on what I have lost and on what I am not or to begin to focus on who I really am and on the gifts that God has given to me as a unique individual.

In the midst of this "crisis of limits," we may find it difficult to pray. We may feel little or no consolation from spiritual exercises, the Mass and sacraments, meditation and spiritual reading. Our faith and trust in God is all that we have, and even this has become a kind of darkness, lacking in consolation. There is a chastening, a purification, taking place in our life of faith.

The words that St. Paul wrote to the Corinthians come to mind:

> The trials that you have had to bear are no more than people normally have. You can trust God not to let you be tried beyond your strength, and with any trial he will give you a way out of it and the strength to bear it.
>
> (1 Cor. 10:13)

Trust in God and patient endurance are the way through the dryness and emptiness of this dark night so common in middle age. This night that we undergo is a normal part of the crisis of limits. We need to know that, or we may add guilt and self blame to the difficulties we are already experiencing.

We must surrender ourselves to God and his will for us, believing with all our strength that his grace will be sufficient for us in the midst of trials we are enduring. We must attempt to the best of our ability, to see this pain of emptiness not as abandonment or loss but as a time of purification and growth. The faith to which we cling in the midst of the darkness is itself God's most gracious gift to us.

# PART TWO

# INTEGRATING PRAYER AND PARTICIPATION

# CONTENTS

## *I*

## *RETREAT AND RETURN TO REALITY*

\* \* \*

During retreat, the divine light seems to permeate all human situations, but, when we return home, we see that opposition and ill will, envy and jealousy still persist. The "aroma of sanctity" fades quickly as we are faced with the truth of our human condition. How is it possible not to become discouraged, not to lose faith?

\* \* \*

Imagine yourself in a concert hall. The musicians assemble on the stage. Soon the discordant sounds of practice runs fill the auditorium. As the conductor lifts his baton, the audience grows still. Hushed expectancy gives way to sound. The music soars and speaks of life—its heights and depths, its shadows and lights. The musicians are one with their instruments. During the performance, a sense of harmony pervades conductor, players, listeners; they honor the composer whose music is able to raise men to transcendent heights.

When the concert ends, this harmonious whole breaks into component parts. "Heavenly artists" become human again! The pianist relaxes, leans back, and stifles a yawn. The cellist bends over unceremoniously and picks up a bulgy pocketbook lying beside her chair. Members of the "enraptured" audience begin leaving before the conductor has taken his final bows.

I don't want to see the pianist as a middle-aged, balding man; I don't want the cellist to take me back to the world of keys and kleenex or the anxious crowd to remind me that my car is parked in a bad corner of the lot. On second thought, why can't I love the tired humanity of the musicians, who are tired because they have given so much? As I am carried out with the crowd and back into the current of everyday, I try to keep alive the impact of the symphony.

I feel renewed by the force and beauty of these past two hours. The perfection of the music has sharpened my senses. I hear the sounds of voices and traffic; I feel the pulse of ordinary life; I try to appreciate it in a new way because it is the raw material from which music is distilled. I want to hold on to my recharged perceptions, my sense of completeness and harmony.

A retreat, like an evening's concert, is not the whole of life. It is a time of refreshment. It is not meant to lead me out of life but to be an entrance into the heart of reality through greater knowledge of self, through opening up to a fuller potential. It is this augmented self that I bring back to my everyday routine.

If I am fortunate enough to undergo a stirring experience during a retreat, I can draw upon this as an incentive for further growth. God graces me during this time with a heightened sense of his love and concern. He gives me the kind of spiritual boost I need every so often to help me live with peace and joy.

If I come home so filled with fervor that I lose sight of the pace and particulars of those around me, I may misuse the benefits of my retreat in impulsive attempts to make others change. God gives his light to each of us in his own time. We can do little to hasten the spiritual unfolding of others except by our prayer, example, and gentle response. If God wills, they may spontaneously open up to us as channels of his grace.

When we carry our retreat experience with us in the form of greater patience toward those who oppose or exclude us, we will indeed hold on to the "aroma of sanctity." We are able to accept peacefully the tensions and differences that occur in any community. To live with charity amid opposition and misunderstanding is to do the bidding of our Lord.

When we want to preserve the significant moments of family life, we take pictures. Christenings, birthdays, vacations, and like events are fixed on film. Similarly, when we keep a journal during retreat, it serves to recall in what way we were touched by God; it preserves these valued moments so we can return to them again and again.

The poet Wordsworth stopped to listen to the young reaper singing at her work and noted:

> The music in my heart I bore,
> Long after it was heard no more.

Looking back on another special moment, he wrote in "I Wandered Lonely as a Cloud,"

> For oft, when on my couch I lie
> In vacant or in pensive mood,
> They flash upon that inward eye
> Which is the bliss of solitude;
> And then my heart with pleasure fills,
> And dances with the daffodils.

Wordsworth had no tape of the reaper's song; he did not pick any of the daffodils, but both experiences remained in his heart, in his "inward eye."

The inner eye perceives what is given; it guides our return to outer action and community concern. As John Donne wrote in his *Devotions Upon Emergent Occasions:*

> No man is an island, entire of itself; every man is a piece of the continent, a part of the main. If a clod be washed away by the sea, Europe is the less, as well as if a promontory

were, as well as if a manor of thy friend's or of thine own were: any man's death diminishes me because I am involved in mankind, and therefore never send to know for whom the bell tolls; it tolls for thee.

Donne is saying we must not separate ourselves from the "flesh and blood" of our life situation. If we step aside momentarily, it is only for the sake of bringing the "continent" of our concern back to its deepest source in Christ.

Ill will, opposition, envy and jealousy must be laid at his feet; our efforts alone will not resolve them. These problems live on in all of us; we all need to be redeemed.

The illusion of retreat can be that I leave this "flesh" of human life behind when I enter into solitude. To correct this deception, it is good to recall Christ's words to those who wanted to tear out the weeds planted by the enemy. "No, because when you weed out the darnel you might pull up the wheat with it. Let them both grow till the harvest: and at harvest time I shall say to the reapers: First collect the darnel and tie it in bundles to be burned, then gather the wheat into my barn." (Mt. 29-30)

Retreat should be an integrating experience in which I allow my whole life—the wheat and the weeds—to be brought into intimate encounter with God. I bring before him the boss I can't stand, the distressing conflict between me and my neighbor, the explosive anger that hurts unnecessarily. Retreat is not an escapist trick that removes me from the weeds of enmity and the disintegrating experiences of life. It should not make me believe that utopia is at hand.

A truly Christian retreat puts me in tune with my call to imitate Christ by living his total Paschal Mystery. This mystery implies the moment to moment passing over from death to new life. If I return from retreat with the expectation of instant perfection, I cease to live the Paschal

Mystery. The human condition is such that the light of the spirit is always dimmed by the darkness of sin.

Life is a dynamic tension of good and evil. Christ accepted this world enough to give his life for our sake. He entered the real world of beauty and ugliness, of trust and betrayal, of humility and pride. He wanted people to bring their day to day worlds to him, to share their situation, as it was, with him, to seek salvation from him, and not from their own projects of perfection.

Fishermen brought to him their concerns about the catch; tax collectors the scandal and hatred of their position; Magdalene her tarnished nature. The leper brought his leprosy; the blind man, his blindness; the crippled, his broken limbs; a mother, her concern for the future of her two sons. Peter brought his lack of courage and his impetuous nature. All came to him to be healed. All felt the life and death, light and shadow, harmony and tension dynamics that mark the fully human life.

To reflect on my life without integrating these polarities is a subtle escape that "diminishes me." I am not accepting that "I am involved in mankind"—in all of mankind's mystery, redeemed not by our merits but by Christ's love.

In the Gospel account of the Transfiguration, Luke tells us that Jesus took Peter, James and John to the mountain to pray. (Lk. 9:28-36) He invited them to retreat with him, away from the crowds, away from their familiar environment and the routine of daily life. Here they experienced the glory and majesty of Christ in a totally new way. This Jesus, who walked the dusty roads with them, was suddenly transfigured: his face became radiant, his clothes dazzling white. Caught up in the awesomeness of the experience, Peter wanted to remain there, to continue living in this ecstasy. However, a few moments later, Jesus stood before them stripped of glory and radiance. Everything around them was as it was before.

During retreat, I am often like Peter. I tell the Lord that it is good to be here, away from community problems and obligations. I have time to pray and reflect, to be more open to the Lord's message for me and his action in my life. Like Peter, I want to cling to this experience of deeper intimacy and to continue living in this state.

By returning to the ordinariness of life "in the valley," Jesus tells us that it is not possible to remain on the level of heightened religious experience. He invites us to return to our familiar environment, to integrate within our daily situation what has been revealed to us during retreat.

It is not easy to do so because we tend to isolate our retreat experience from concrete living where we no longer have as much time to reflect and pray. What was so clear during retreat slowly seems to disappear. Life becomes more complicated; we are disillusioned when we fail and the euphoria fades.

A quiet return to the Gospels makes us realize that the disciples too failed many times after witnessing the Transfiguration. They were limited like us. Problems such as duplicity and pettiness persist despite the retreats people make. Strengthened and enriched by the experience of deeper intimacy with Christ, we can become more accepting of these frailties and feel merciful toward the human condition.

The vital message of our retreat is thus the message of the Transfiguration: "Listen to him." (Lk. 9: 36) By learning to listen to Jesus in the "now" of daily life, we begin to live out the true benefits of retreat. The mountain top moment can become the background of our daily activities in the valley below. The heightened experience is not lost, for the more we listen to him, the more we are able to integrate what we hear into the art of daily living.

## II

## *ASSESSING THE REAL SITUATION*

* * *

We are open to reality on varying levels, ranging from a high degree of awareness to near oblivion of the real situation. How can we learn to listen to reality so that we can assess the situation properly and prudently?

* * *

Simple situations test the quality of my awareness if I am alert to them. Suppose it has been raining for days. I am tired of the drab weather. One morning I stop for a moment to watch the bubble created as a drop of rain falls on a puddle and ripples away. Soon I notice the esthetic effect of rain falling not only into the puddles but on everything else. Rain drops form puddles that converge into rivulets that run to the edge of the street and down the hill into the river. My thoughts expand to take into account the life-giving quality of water, its cleansing effects. The rain may perhaps remind me of the unity of all men, for all are in need of it.

Had I chosen not to be attentive to the rain in this meditative way, I would have missed something, whereas my reflective presence to the life-giving water opens me to the many meanings it may give rise to.

When we take time to be present to our situation, we discover that our perception is deepened; our way of thinking is enlarged. We learn to watch, to wait, to weigh. We look with a fresh eye. We penetrate beyond the obvious.

To see is to love. How do we see what is there? How do

we have access to reality in its many meanings? The answer is that we usually don't. We are all blinded by our practical projects and prejudices, our fears, likes and dislikes. We see but with our own brand of colored vision.

Reality is all that is; we must accept that our perception encompasses only part of it according to our limitations. The more we are conscious of these limitations, the clearer our view of reality will be.

For instance, if I know that I am a dominating type of person, that I tend to take control of situations, this self knowlege will help me in assessing a negative response I get from a friend, who may feel threatened by me. Without this realization I would not have been aware that my particular personality is what evoked his resentment.

Therefore, our first task in developing the art of appraisal of the real situation is to know who we are—that basic lifelong pursuit on which all else depends. Everything we observe is filtered through the self. Often, in the pain and discomfort of focusing on our flaws and faulty vision, we reach an awakening that helps us to listen better to who we are in the situations we have to cope with daily.

Without self insight, we run the risk of cutting life into predictable shapes and sizes that suit our prejudices. Honest reflection can show us the unexamined influences and assumptions that underlie our view of the world. Indeed, the more aware we are of the ways in which we are closed, the more open we become to reality.

Along with growth in self awareness, we should attend to awakening from the complacency that threatens all of us. If we are content with our narrow view, we may not risk the enlightenment God asks. It is certainly easier to live in "tunnel vision," content with our little cave, than to listen to God's calling us into the light.

To add new dimensions to our life requires discipline and the courage to see what is really there. Only in seeing things as they are is it possible to participate truly in life.

Has a friend ever asked you, "Are you really listening to me?" When you ask him to explain what he means by this question, he may say that he feels as if part of you were not present. You were listening to snatches of what he was saying. He feels as if you were only vaguely aware of him.

When we do not listen, we may experience a certain emptiness; it evidences our own lack of presence to the situation. Instead of being filled with the sound of life, we echo only an endless monologue of what we are thinking and feeling.

Listening implies a total attentiveness. I bring to it all that I am and allow the "silent voice" of the situation to appeal to me. This voice can only be heard by one who stops and listens with his whole being.

Now I enter wholeheartedly into conversation with my friend. Not only do I hear what he has to tell me; I am also aware of the love and trust that exist between us, rarely spoken but always present.

Modern man is faced with such a mass of input that he must screen himself from bombardment and organize some of it into a reflex response. Unfortunately, eating, dressing, walking, and so on, lose their flavor when they are only and always lived as automatic reflexes.

It would be beneficial for us to break sometimes with habitual patterns, and allow ourselves to be conscious of the here and now—of the way in which we speak or move about. Certainly a gulped breakfast taken while reading the paper is less desirable spiritually than gratefully savoring the gift of warm eggs and buttered toast. The first, fast way often becomes an unnecessary habit.

In the same manner, we group large portions of diffuse information together and label them: Plants, Furniture, Love, Hatred . . . Some categories are a help in assimilating reality in a peripheral way but others are blinding. They close us to the rich variety of each particular person, event and thing and may lead to ill-founded conclusions and false assumptions.

Thorton Wilder's play *Our Town* attempts to find the value, above all price, of the smallest event in daily life. Emily, having just died, asks and is allowed to return to a day in her life . . . her twelfth birthday. As she relives the day and watches herself going through it, she experiences the anguish of seeing how she and her family, basically loving yet typically human and forgetful, fail to really "look at one another." This sad fact causes Emily to beg to be taken back "up the hill" to her grave before the day is over.

> "But first: Wait!", she cries. "One more look. Good-by, Good-by world . . . Mama and Papa. Good-by to clocks ticking . . . and Mama's sunflowers and food and coffee. And newly ironed dresses and hot baths . . . and sleeping and waking up. Oh, earth, you're too wonderful for anybody to realize you."

Each of us needs in some way to experience a similar return to life. We need to develop a reverent presence to reality, and a gentle desire to understand the directives that come through each situation.

It is the artist who teaches us how to see. I know a painter who leads his students to a field where he asks them to sit about in the grass and take note of some small object, a leaf, an ant, a twig. He tells them to close their eyes and completely relax for a few seconds. Then he asks them to study their chosen object intensely with their whole heart and mind to the exclusion of all else. Notice that he has them clear their minds first in a kind of self emptying. Only after these steps are they ready to observe their subjects for drawing. Such meditative seeing ought to be imitated by all of us.

We do so much looking but see less and less, so much listening and hear less and less, reading voluminously and appropriating little.

Reality is an expression of the Divine, inexhaustible in its richness. What we receive from it depends on God's grace and the quality of our presence to it. In dying to ourselves—to our fears, desires, needs, prejudices, defenses—all of which distort reality, we can grasp with St. Paul " . . . the breadth and the length, the height and the depth; until, knowing the love of Christ, which is beyond all knowledge, you are filled with the utter fullness of God." (Ep. 3: 18-19)

## III

## TENSION OF CONFLICTING CALLS

\* \* \*

I feel within myself a peculiar tension, offset, I think, by two apparently conflicting calls. The Martha in me wants a busy professional life, the Mary desires contemplation. How can I reconcile these conflicting sides of myself?

\* \* \*

When was the last time I left my watch at home? Did the hours not unfold as usual? My "watchless" day was well spent. It also taught me a valuable lesson about the unnecessary tension caused by "time boundness."

In contrast to this enslavement to scheduling, I may recall the "timelessness" that goes with a quiet day at the shore. True, it was necessary to make time for this timelessness, but let's consider the real question. The problem posed seems less a matter of tension between two apparently opposite calls and more a matter of assigning priorities.

Moments of reflection ought to be woven into my day as a whole. They ought not to be "special slots" I have to "make time for."

Few of us can "get away from it all." What we must try to do instead is "get more deeply into what is there," that is, to live closer and closer to God so that we can sense his presence shining through our profession. Obeying his holy will ought to form the ever present background of my office or teaching schedule, of my balancing accounts or correcting class papers, of my attending conventions or preparing lectures.

The tensions between time and the Eternal, that usually grow out of a professional situation, arise from a split between the "beat the clock" approach toward getting things done and the desire to relax, unwind, and reflect before God. The commitments I find myself responsible for often cannot be altered, but I can change my attitude.

Just what is this contemplative way I seek? Is it merely a mountain top experience or is it the everyday ability to hold on for a moment to what I am doing, to look at myself in my present situation and to ponder the mystery that my life is a channel God uses to build his world?

This reflective hold on reality in its Holy Origin is not limited to set times. It is an attitude of living fully the "now" moment. It cannot happen if I am thinking ahead to what I must do next or "holding off" until I have time for "pure" contemplation. That time may come in monasteries, but it seldom comes for the person in the world.

The hands of the clock are always moving in endless circles of seconds, minutes, hours, days, years. They seem to go nowhere, but they travel at great speed. Life moves at an ever quickened pace the older we grow. The habit of living more reflectively does not mean throwing my watch away, being late for everything, passively flowing with whatever comes along. It is simply a valuable means of adding depth and direction to each moment of my day as I read in it the richness of God's real presence.

The problem of missing the connection is wider than we may think. A friend, burdened with a heavy schedule and the emotional strain of a family crisis, once wrote:

I've thought a lot about the meaning of life this past month —operating as I've had to, under lots of pressure, feeling the pinch of time or lack of it. The quality of life, I discover, depends so much on the small, seemingly insignificant, choices we make. I see more and more that who I am is of surpassing value to what I do. I find myself praying not *outside of* work, as I used to do, but *in the midst of* things. I bring the whole of my day to the light of the Holy.

This person seems to have found the way to respond to the call to action *and* to her desire to spend more time in prayer. She responds to this twofold call by pausing, however briefly, and reflecting on her situation in God's light. She could not say *yes* to prayer and *no* to the professional and familial demands placed on her. She had to reconcile both calls in a deepening awareness of the value of her being. This awareness then renews her doing. She continued:

I have grown in gentleness toward and respect for myself. Somehow I find this attitude spilling over into my relationships with my family and at the office. God has really been with me. I smile at the way I used to act: convinced that a meeting could not go on without me; that an office project would never get done unless I did it. What arrogance! Then, following the same style, I would organize time to pray, trying to control God the way I controlled others and myself.

Now I strive to listen in humble openness to myself and my situation. I take into account the demands of body, psyche, and spirit; I try to uncover the unconscious persuaders of ambition, guilt, or fear that blind me to God's call in this situation. When necessary I choose to dive headlong into my work, even increasing time for activity, but in the background I leave room for God to enter in. A simple prayer like "Come, Lord Jesus," is always possible no matter how busy I am. Little wonder I used to live in unbearable tension.

This person has learned to recognize and respond rightly to the twofold call. Now she finds the Martha moments ideal opportunities for being creatively faithful to Christ in the Mary-like center of her being.

A misunderstanding of availability makes me sometimes take on too much. It is as if I want to alleviate singlehandedly the suffering, ignorance and difficulties of the world. In my classroom I feel obliged to implement every new program. I volunteer for extra-curricular activities. I petition for safer transportation for handicapped children. At home I try anxiously to solve family fights, internally and with the neighborhood.

Though I subject my efforts to frequent self-evaluation, I always find more to do—calling my exhaustion the "fruits of Christian charity." I soothe my conscience this way rather than admitting my "savior complex." Secretly, I live with the attitude: "If only I work hard enough, I can eventually solve all the problems of my world, work and family."

Caught in this bind, I feel increasingly responsible for the ignorance and suffering I see all around me. I oblige myself to relieve these needs by tireless work. Any sign of failure is extremely depressing. I measure growth by the result of *my* efforts alone.

Despite my good will, service in this case becomes an obstacle to grace rather than a channel of charity. My work becomes an idol I worship to the exclusion of the true God who loves me in my littleness.

Exhaustion may make it impossible after a while to exert any more effort. Now I may have to stop long enough to hear God's direction for my life. Prayer and meditation help me to appraise the duties I must justly fulfill and to give up those which support the "savior complex."

As I come to know and accept my gifts and limits, I am more confident of assessing my obligations in God's light.

In prayerful presence to my Creator, I am reminded of my role in the world: to be his servant, inspiring others by my relaxed and joyful incarnation of Christ within the limits of my abilities. Tension and exhaustion do not signify the faith life that is my primary obligation.

I need, therefore, continually to evaluate my pursuits in light of this prayerful call. Open to the word of God, I am less likely to take on activities that may not be his will for me but only a symptom of my willfulness.

When work interferes with spiritual growth, it becomes empty of its real worth in the Kingdom. As I drift farther away from God, I cease to incarnate his Spirit in my culture. Instead of pointing to values that transcend immediate success, I bind myself to service of the "false gods" of efficiency, success, and maximum production. The tension that mounts acts often as a catalyst motivating me to examine my life—to test the "metal" of which I am made.

In science there is a law that states: anything left to itself will tend toward equilibrium. Metal is supposed to possess a certain quality of elasticity. A given amount of stress or tension can be applied to a piece of metal, and unless the metal is overstressed, it will again assume its original shape. The breaking point or the rupture stage is reached when the limit of elasticity is surpassed.

To refrain from stretching a metal beyond the limits of its endurance requires a certain discipline. Achieving a balance between my apostolic endeavors and my desire for prayer requires discipline as well.

If I allow my profession to take precedence, a breaking point will be reached—the result being a distorted Christian existence. It takes some slowing down and much reflectiveness to remind myself that Christ is calling me to build my house not on the shifting sands of success but on the rock of recollection.

Prayer, in short, must be the mainstay of my professional and apostolic life. The many seemingly wasted moments that arise in an activity-filled day can be times to regain a sense of my primary commitment. These in-between moments may be my bridge to inwardness, which crosses over into the outer life.

Once my presence becomes centered in the Divine Presence, moments of contemplative communion become the sustaining ground of service, just as good soil causes a garden to flourish.

## IV

## INNER PEACE IN THE MIDST OF OUTER AGITATION

\* \* \*

Spiritual writers speak of having a "core of inner peace" in the midst of outer agitation, of recollection in the midst of work. How can we be at peace inwardly while outwardly agitated or overloaded with work?

\* \* \*

A pond in winter. A skater pivoting on the ice. A solitary person day after day practicing a figure-eight. Turn, reverse, turn—climaxing in a vigorous yet graceful spin. The pivot ends abruptly. The young man skates off to further perfect his skill.

What is the secret of such a feat? It is the skater's ability to focus on one object. As long as he concentrates on one thing, a tree, a fence, a point on the distant horizon, he will maintain his balance.

I too need a point on which to focus if I am to preserve equanimity. As the skater's inner calm is not touched by his whirlwind activity, so too I need a "core of inner peace" enabling me to begin each new action with my feet firmly on the ground.

The activities of professional life can reach whirlwind proportions. The tension of nervous strain begins to affect me. Energies diffuse. The direction my life takes is unsteady. There seems to be no stopping. Now is the time to ask myself if I have lost my point of focus. If so, it is wise to fix my gaze on Christ, the source of calming union.

To maintain a core of inner peace requires that I look within myself to find God, for he is my axis. Such prayer gives me a chance to gather in the circles of activity in which I feel myself dispersed. I look at my involvements and try to see them in the light of the Divine Will for me. For the sake of inner calm, I let go of peripheral concerns.

I may find that the cause of my agitation is a shift from God as center to self as center. To be most deeply at peace, I must heed the words of the psalmist:

> In God, I find shelter; rely on him
> people, at all times;
> unburden your hearts to him,
> God is a shelter for us.
> (Ps. 62: 8)

Only the Lord can lay to rest our restlessness in him. Peace is essentially his sheltering gift.

A friend lost her mother after a long, painful illness. She is an outgoing excitable person, who must have felt acutely the strain of nursing her aged mother, yet she carried on devotedly. After her mother died, she was for others a model of serenity. What happened to her?, her friends asked. "I learned not to seek for the answer why mother had to suffer so but to ask only for trust and strength. When the pressures got to be too much and there was no where else to turn, I called out to God in my desperation. The peace I feel is his own gift of himself to me. It is not of my doing."

If I find that my life is generally lived in some state of agitation, I cannot wish away the stress. Pressures of work and the hurried pace inflict strain upon my physical and emotional being. In the midst of this stress, I can always ask God to give me his peace. I can bring the agitations and concerns of my day before him and look at them in his light. I can pray:

> Lord, I have an important meeting with the building supervisor today. Whatever we talk about, whenever we speak together, I get defensive. Take up this hardness of heart. Help me to realize that he is human too, that all is in your hands. Whether I succeed or fail, let your will be done.

Such a prayer helps me to realize that this meeting agitates me because I may be holding on too tightly to my own ideas. I can begin, with his grace, to let go.

On some days it takes longer than on others to come to restful presence before God. I may need to take a walk in the evening to quiet myself or talk out my concerns with a friend. These actions help me to recollect myself physically and emotionally. I should not consider them unnecessary or say that I cannot find the time.

When I come before God in recollected presence, he will lay to rest my restlessness. I may still feel my pressure rising when I go to the meeting, but perhaps I will be more able to stay calm. I may not find my problems solved in the way I would like, but at least I can find that center of myself where my will is one with his. Agitation lets up and I begin to live from my center. There I am one with God. There I find peace.

Though Adam and Eve lived in union with God, free from anxiety and fear, they chose to defy him. As a result they found themselves experiencing tensions not known before. Their initial unity was disrupted; their spirit, once free, now found itself bound in limitations.

Such is our inheritance: an inner desire for equanimity and peace hampered by a strong tendency to isolate ourselves from God. Thus we become fragmented.

As spirit self, we reach beyond imagination, reasoning,

emotions and needs, toward that which we perceive as eternal. As vital and ego self, we are bound to imagination, reasoning, emotions and needs, often in conflict. Because of these dynamic forces within us, agitation is inevitable.

There are three ways in which we can handle these forces. We can let the vital and ego levels "run wild," unleashed and isolated from the influence of the spirit self; or we can repress them, deny their existence, and keep them under cover while they smoulder beneath; or we can choose wisely, to integrate these resistant feelings and functions into the gentle flow of our spirit-life through faith and the knowledge that we have been redeemed. Under this unifying aspect life remains a mosaic of many pieces, but each fits together to form a meaningful whole.

Perhaps a revolving cartwheel might serve as an illustration of this third way. When the wheel is turning slowly, it is obvious that the hub is the axis around which everything rotates. As it gathers speed, however, all the activity seems to move towards the periphery. The further out it goes, the more agitated the action. At first glance it even seems as if the movements at the fringe are isolated from the rest of the wheel. Meanwhile, the movement of the hub is so effortless, it becomes almost imperceptible. It is, however, the dynamic center that keeps the wheel rotating and grounded.

Faith and my inner core of peace are like the hub of the wheel. They keep me grounded and going even when my life becomes marginal and separated from its center in God.

I can remember walking home from school and getting caught in a blinding snowstorm. The stinging cold wind and the wet flakes penetrated my skin and sent icy chills all over my body. As swiftly as possible I sought refuge in the cozy warmth of my living room where a fire crackled in the old stone hearth. I had come in out of the turbulence to a haven of peace and security. I was still aware of the agitation outdoors, but I had found calm in the midst of the storm.

Similarly, we may speak of a calm region in the soul to which we retire for refuge from the outer tumult of life. This still region in the depths of our being is not a physical place like our living room. It is a spiritual center of peace in Christ, even in the midst of the agitation of daily life.

What Jesus promised us was not a peace without tension; rather he bequeathed to us a peace that would surpass understanding. It would endure regardless of surface disruptions. This peace is experienced when we keep God's word and obey his will.

United with God on this level of the deepest self, we are still aware of the pressing agitation of many problems, but we are able to see these agitations as part of his caring for us. These concerns become means of closer union with the suffering Christ. Maybe we will not understand all that God asks. Yet, in faith and trust, we can say "Yes" to the mystery he desires to work out in us.

When we recognize God's will in our daily activities and anxieties, we are stilled. His peace surpasses our anxious concerns. We feel able to pray once again.

Lord, along the river bank, the reeds of the marshland are tossed and ruffled by the wind. How often I've watched storms blow in with their towering force and batter the unprotected reeds flat to the ground in a fury of wind and rain. Yet, when the wind dies down and I stroll by the water's edge, I am amazed at the triumph of these fragile plants. There they are, upright and erect in the morning breeze. How can a reed bend so low and yet refuse to break? Is it not because far below the surface of the ground, in the silent depths of its roots, the reed is invulnerable. Even when the wind beats the hardest, the roots sleep on in the depths of the marshland.

I think of myself as a wind-tossed reed. At times I find the world a stormy place. My employers are demanding, my colleagues deceptive, all my best efforts seem to be aborted. I feel miserable in the face of defeat, hurt by a lack of understanding, levelled like the reed by powers that threaten me on all sides. I become harsh with myself and with others. I want to whip my foolishness into shape. All I succeed in doing is to become more and more agitated, filled with self hate and bitter feelings towards others.

Left to myself in the midst of a storm, I close my eyes and think of you. The disciples were caught just this way on a storm tossed lake until they awakened you and you calmed the waves. You calmed their fears too, though you reprimanded them for their lack of faith. You tell me that though I fear, if I have faith, I am not demolished. In the core of my being is your peace.

You have made me a unique person. Though the contribution I have to make is limited, it is my unrepeatable offering of self through you to the world.

A certain peace comes over me. In this moment of inwardness, I recognize anew the value of being who I am. I open my eyes to the world again. I am erect like a reed, at peace with myself and with you. From this inner peace there flows a new willingness to reach out to others.

But I have found more than just myself in this inner core. Below the troubles of my mind and the emotional up-surges, I descend into the spiritual center of my soul. It is difficult to get there, but I allow myself to slip down, to let go . . . knowing that in the sacred core of self I am held, sustained in an Infinite Peace that surpasses understanding.

Here, at a level below all agitation, I am encompassed by you. In the Infinite Stillness which surrounds me, agitation disappears. In the peace of this moment, muscles relax; my mind is free of preoccupying thoughts; the whole of me is enveloped in the sustaining power of your peace.

When I return to work, Lord, I know that I shall be a
bearer of peace because I have been in touch with the
Source of Peace himself.

## V

## SPIRITUALITY AND INVOLVEMENT WITH SOCIAL ISSUES

\* \* \*

How can we reconcile our longing for the spiritual life with the trend to become more involved in social issues?

\* \* \*

An old gardener was planting rose bushes. Intent on his work, he hoed the earth, added fertilizer, pulled out weeds. Watching him, one gradually became aware of a rhythm in his work. Every so often he stepped back and surveyed what he had done. It seemed as if he were trying to determine how effective was the arrangement of new bushes in the garden and how well they were positioned to grow.

What struck me was his complete involvement simultaneously in both dimensions of his work—the manual labor itself and the contemplative gaze upon its results. To him both acts were necessary to achieve the perfection he sought.

An oft quoted passage from *The Little Prince* by Antoine de Saint Exupery comes to mind here: "It is the time you have wasted for your rose that makes your rose so important." The word "wasted" implies time spent in a nonutilitarian way. As the fox in *The Little Prince* says: "It is only with the heart that one can see rightly; what is essential is invisible to the eye."

In my concern to be involved and of service, I can, therefore, ask myself do I lose sight of the basic truth that I am a finite being who depends on God for everything I do?

Is the fatigue I feel a result of honest work or is it a sign of needless worry?

The more demanding a task is, the more necessary it is to look at it from a distance. This standing back allows me to deepen my understanding of it. It is the contemplative perspective that helps me to see what God wants me to do, and not the slogan that "I can do anything I put my mind to."

God calls most of us to be ordinary laborers in his vineyard without heroics, even without major sacrifice. We are asked to put him first, to move through each day somehow in touch with him. How often we are presented with the opportunity to listen with patience to someone in search of support. We need not wait for an emergency nor look for extraordinary means to do God's will.

In the initial stages of involvement, we are usually so preoccupied with its demands that we have little time to pray and reflect on our lives. They are too full. As the work routine sets in and we gradually adjust to these dimensions, we begin to take a closer look at ourselves and at the issues in which we are involved.

A vague feeling of emptiness inside—despite the flurry of activity outside—leads us to rediscover the need for a deeper spiritual life to sustain us. Christ has to be the center. It is in living through him that we witness to the world. Our presence to Jesus permeates our participation in these works. We do not abandon our activities in society; we bring to them the richness that flows from a spiritual life.

Instant integration is not possible. It takes time to balance wisely activity and recollection. This balance weaves its way slowly through the whole of life. Priorities are reordered; blind spots removed; values restored—all with the help of grace. Inspiration and incarnation become part of everyday life. The world of spirit is wed to the world of fact.

Always the balance has to be there. Only if I bring Christ with me can I find him in the market place. In other words, the deeper effectiveness of social involvement corresponds to the depth of my spiritual life. I cannot give to others what I do not possess myself.

In my daily union with the Lord, I realize my complete dependence on him. I can only succeed in the market place to the degree that I realize that I am there to do God's work, not merely to see tangible results or to get immediate rewards.

Candles come in various shapes and sizes. Whether they are used for decoration or for light in an emergency, all candles possess a common element: the wick. Small and insignificant as it may appear, the wick makes the candle what it is. Without it, a candle remains a useless piece of wax.

Like the candle, I too need a wick, the wick of a deepening spiritual life. Without this dimension, my involvement risks becoming mere activism. But how can I nourish this prayer life, keep alive this wick, in the midst of so many commitments? I find a clue in the Gospels.

Christ, too, was involved in a life of service. However, he knew how and when to take the time to nourish his life in moments of exclusive presence to the Father in prayer. The Evangelists tell us that Jesus repeatedly disappeared from the crowd to go off by himself to pray. He had to make time in his life for moments of reflection. In these moments he discovered the will of the Father for him and found the inner strength necessary to live out his will.

Jesus tells me by his example that I need to take time periodically to slow down my hectic pace, to enter into the depths of my being and there to get in touch with the true self I am—with Christ in me. During these moments of quiet reflection and prayer, I slowly discover the Father's will, in tune as it is with my unique individuality and concrete situation.

As I develop the ability to discover his appeal, the apparent opposition between spiritual life and worldly involvement diminishes. My primary concern becomes the living out of God's will as it is manifested in my situation. Gradually this inspirational dimension permeates all my activities.

Just as a candle is of little value without a wick, so my work life risks losing its witness value without a deepening of the contemplative dimension.

## VI

## PRAYER AND THE PROBLEM OF FATIGUE

\* \* \*

How often we hear people say—even after a night's sleep—"I'm tired . . . " Would you comment on fatigue in general and particularly its bearing on the life of prayer?

\* \* \*

It goes without saying that we cannot pray and sleep at the same time. If I rise in the morning, stumble around in semi-consciousness, and then try to pray, it is no wonder that I cannot stay awake.

Fatigue dulls our attention and powers of concentration; it causes us to be irritable and weakens our sense of resoluteness. Trying to meditate at such a time only results in frustration.

"Morning fatigue" may be another way of saying "not full awake." Still morning may be the only time I have for meditation. I rise hurriedly, dress quickly, swallow breakfast, stop at Church on the way to work, kneel or sit, begin to pray, then promptly drift off to sleep.

Such prayer is hardly comparable to what Thomas Merton describes as an inner awareness of God's direct presence or an awakening of one's inner self. This awakening requires that my physical body be sufficiently stimulated to listen to the stirrings of God in my deepest self.

Fatigue arises for different reasons. The first and most obvious is due to not enough rest to restore the body after its normal activity. Many of us take on more than we can manage. Regardless of our altruistic motives, if we continue to augment an already crowded schedule, we are bound to lose our effectiveness and perhaps our health as well.

Certainly when we ignore the signals from our bodies that point toward tension and excessive fatigue, we are disregarding God's will speaking in our vital limits. Eating properly, getting adequate fresh air, sleep and exercise are basics for a sound style of life.

Fatigue can result from psychological reasons. There are monotonous winter days when I wonder how I will stay awake after the last class to finish assignments, to say nothing of going to chapel for prayer. I feel dejected and listless. A glass of milk and a nap seem more in order than trying to study or pray. I decide to go home. As I open the lock, I find some letters the postman has slipped under the door. "At least I got some mail," I think, not only "some" mail but a special letter from a dear friend and an invitation to come visit her in two weeks. Instant cure. No headache, no fatigue, no blues. I am alive with enthusiasm that carries over to the study and prayer I was going to postpone.

My initial weariness was not imaginary. The fact was my ordinary routine had fallen into drudgery. Fatigue was rooted in spiritual listlessness, in a lack of meaning. Boredom and a general sort of ennui had crept into my life.

Many of us experience a similar slugginess. Some are exceptionally vulnerable to the noise and clatter of modern life. Others are less adept at handling resentments and pettiness. Many become tense with the pressures of competition; they are disappointed by their lack of achievement and overwhelmed by the materialistic thrust that urges us to have what is beyond our reach. Still others move through life disgruntled with the place and time in which God has called them to live.

All of these forces, and many others, cause us some degree of anger. I wait for a friend; he is late. Someone rejects me; the response is anger. One of the major manifestations of either accumulated or severe anger is depression. There are few in our culture who do not suffer some measure of depression—the depression that flows from anger.

Nothing brings on fatigue faster than depression. Even during the most frenetic schedule or compulsive overworking we get recharged. But depression empties us of vitality. It is a state of withdrawal, a form of giving up. If we cannot pull out, we may slip into despair. Sleep is a welcome reprieve, but as long as we remain depressed even sleep cannot replenish us.

Whether we suffer major depressions from overwhelming and unresolved angers or mild ones due to the ordinary pressures and disappointments of daily life, depression is a state of isolation. It seems to cut us off from the awareness of God. We are filled with self, with our problems, our solutions or lack of them.

Like loneliness, depression is an inward movement. We cannot be present to the Lord in repressed anger; neither can we be present to him in the cloud of fatigue that accompanies it.

The causes of psychological fatigue have to be dealt with on two levels. Rest is essential in healing both physical and psychological fatigue, but equally necessary is a look at the reasons. It is not a matter of mental gymnastics but of quiet listening to God. In this context, fatigue is a call to examine my life and affirm once again its primary goal of intimacy with him.

I begin by sitting still and taking note of how tense I am: wrinkled forehead, clenched jaw, rigid neck. I focus on the reasons for my tension. Realizing my limits in dealing with whatever difficulties life brings is never easy. Nor is the next step: consciously relaxing and letting go. I must surrender to God all the tiredness and the failure I feel. He speaks to me through my body, in my fears, in my unresolved problems, my unconscious requests, my lack of gratitude, my jealousies. Whether I am flaccid or in a frenzy, he will hear my cry.

My course involves both meditative self reflection and surrender to God's care. Without this trust, the alternative is grim: a life of mediocrity, tension, boredom and fatigue. I join the ranks of the alienated and abandoned, whose wreckage litters our culture. In faith I hear his words:

"Come to me, all you who labor and are overburdened, and I will give you rest. Shoulder my yoke and learn from me, for I am gentle and humble of heart, *and you will find rest for your souls.* Yes, my yoke is easy and my burden light."

(Mt. 11: 28-30)

## VII

## *RECOVERING RELIGIOUS ATTITUDES*

\* \* \*

Is there any way to recover the religious attitudes of joy, wonder, gratitude that seemed more prevalent in the past? Can the self-centered, uncharitable and demanding person give witness to Christ?

\* \* \*

Just as good ground is necessary to liberate the blossom from the seed, so too a receptive heart is necessary to liberate the religious attitudes hidden in the Word.

Joy, wonder and gratitude are attitudes in which the Word can mature and bear fruit. Why do these qualities seem absent from our lives? Perhaps because we live in a period that places so much emphasis on productivity that we may have lost sight of the Word from whence all apostolic activity must issue.

Like the seed sown among thorns, the Word may have been choked off by our anxiety over the demands of an active life. Preoccupation with professional competence has led us to overdevelop our active, aggressive qualities at the expense of these more receptive ones.

Our tendency is to totalize professionalism. Joy, wonder and gratitude have been crowded out by unhappiness and self-centeredness. Competence ceased to be at the service of the Word and became an end in itself.

In Dostoevsky's novel, *The Brothers Karamazov,* a character named Zossima, an elder of the monastery near the village, was prized by the people for his wisdom and sought by many for counsel. Of all those who visited him, Zossima was drawn to the sinful; it seemed to the monk that the greater the sinner, the more he loved him, for these troubled people best represented the human condition.

What witness can such people give? Hope comes when and if the self-centered, demanding person recognizes his faults and his need for a Savior. The Lord looks at his efforts, not at his success, and loves him in his weakness.

Such spiritual transformation is a lifelong process. It cannot be hastened according to my pace. If a person is going to change, he will change in God's time, not in mine. My criticism will do nothing to lighten the burden he already carries. Perhaps the only way he will be freed to experience the attitudes of joy, wonder and gratitude is by meeting in me a reflection of the sympathy and compassion of his Savior.

In the Epistle to the Hebrews, we read about the compassionate high priest who " . . . can sympathize with those who are ignorant or uncertain because he too lives in the limitations of weakness." (Heb. 5:2)

Zossima, the holy man, knew what it was to be gentle with the weak. He knew that God is in charge, not I. I cannot know the struggles going on in the hearts of others, but I can be compassionate when I see signs of the weakness I know I share with them. Perhaps the person I label as uncharitable labels me as judgmental. Both of us need to be redeemed.

Especially sad is the case of a person who is immersed in spiritual opportunities yet does not grow to maturity, who does not radiate the joy, wonder and gratitude that seem to be the spontaneous outgrowth of a life of intimacy with Christ. What has gone wrong?

Many reasons could be given, but one seems pertinent, namely, "spiritless religion." The word itself indicates the root of the problem—to be without spirit. The spirit or core of the person's self seems to die. The spirit center no longer permeates all dimensions of the person's life. The functional aspects may have taken over. At some point the person allowed functionalism to become the motivating force in his life—faithfully following social rules of conduct but without giving these the personal meaning that comes from a life enlightened by the spirit.

Life has become an automatic reaction rather than a spirit-centered response. Because this person's spirit has been denied, he can no longer meet the challenges of his own unfolding nor imbibe the spiritual nourishment the Christian community offers. His life lacks buoyancy. Is there anything that can be done to restore him to a vibrant spiritual life?

When a person finds himself dying for lack of spiritual food, he may find his way back to his own spirit wherein dwells the Holy Spirit—source of all religious attitudes. But there is no one formula for restoration. God works in mysterious ways. It is easy to presume that all Christians should be happy and well adjusted, and for some this may be true, but it is also true that there is a lot of unhappiness in our lives. If we humbly accept this fact, we may also be able to accept our need for salvation.

We can idealize the Christian community, making the community itself the source of our happiness rather than Christ in whom we already exist. In him we humbly accept the limitations that will always be within myself and others due to sin, but we seek as well to reach our fullest potential as saints.

Without this approach we will continue to count on our own strength when all we can count on is the support of the Lord. We may begin to build community on basis of our own self image rather than give glory and praise to God by accepting the limits of our situation.

We are all a fallen people. We will never know what

demons of heredity or history are clinging to the other's heart and impeding his way. We cannot know to what extent his inner vision is distorted by past experiences nor how his unconscious system of defenses works against the call of his deepest self.

All we can see in our brother's life is the cross he is carrying. We cannot know whether suffering is for him a purifying experience or not. Perhaps he has responded generously to the call of grace God has allowed to echo in his life. Maybe he is struggling in spite of repeated failure to overcome his faults. It could be that his life is the result of a series of sinful rejections of God's mercy—but I cannot judge.

He stands as a reminder to me that I may be blind to the plank in my eye as I shake my head over the sight of the splinter that seems to be impeding his vision. (Mt. 7:3-4) Perhaps he is a reminder to all of us that salvation is from the Lord and does not come from spiritual exercises as such. Our only hope is in the mercy of God. It does not depend on our track record of religious achievements.

The life of the most spiritual person in the world would become a curse the moment he rested in satisfied complacency, as if his life were some kind of stock entitling him to the favor of God. When my brother's sad condition reminds me of our common sinfulness, then perhaps he is carrying out a special mission to remind the community of Christians of its need for redemption.

## PART THREE

## LIVING CHRISTIAN COMMUNITY

# CONTENTS

# I

## *BUILDING HUMAN RELATIONS ON TRUST*

\* \* \*

I realize that all human relationships must be built on trust. What do we do when we learn from experience that a person cannot be trusted, when, for example, he reveals a confidence that hurts the reputation of another person?

\* \* \*

Love takes no pleasure in other people's sins but delights in the truth; it is always ready to excuse, to trust, to hope, and to endure whatever comes. (1 Cor. 13:6-7)

When we are not able to trust another because of past experiences, innate common sense seems to demand that in some way we regulate our interactions with this person. There are various levels of trust that operate between people.

Despite the proven inability to trust a person with confidences, we may still trust in his underlying goodness. Our response to him may be varied. We may feel angry, hurt, resentful. A pervasive bitterness may govern our relationship from now on. Once the immediacy of the incident passes over, I need to move beyond these negative responses and seek to follow the words of the Epistle—"ready to excuse, to trust, to hope."

We may distrust the good judgment of the other, but we need not extend this distrust to his whole person. Perhaps in this specific incident he weakened and deserves another chance. I diminish myself if I take pleasure in the weakness of another.

Life is such that we must learn to remain open to the human potential for grace and redemption.

What if I am the one who has lost the trust of others and am now seeking to regain it? Trust is not something I can demand. It is a relationship I earn by my living. It may be either given or received. Whether I am the giver or the receiver of trust, I need to believe in the potency for goodness, honesty and sincerity in each person I meet.

Without this belief in the graced possibilities for goodness in others, I leave them no room for change or growth. I simply put them in a slot labelled "Untrustworthy."

Am I able to take the risk and believe in someone who has on several occasions shown himself untrustworthy? I can do so only if I believe that every human being is a mystery, even to himself, and that no one can predict in advance how grace may move his heart.

Because a person has shown himself to be untrustworthy once, twice or several times, does not mean that he will remain that way forever. Surely the words of Jesus to Peter, when he wanted to know how many times to forgive his brothers, are applicable here: "Not seven, I tell you, but seventy-seven times." (Mt. 18: 21-22)

What kind of trust do we need? St. Paul wrote to the Galatian community about a test of his trust:

> When Cephas [Peter] came to Antioch, however, I opposed him to his face, since he was manifestly in the wrong. His custom had been to eat with the pagans, but after certain friends of James arrived he stopped doing this and kept away from them altogether for fear of the group that insisted on circumcision. (Gal. 2: 11-12)

Peter, in this action, was not trustworthy. Paul drew himself up, responsible to his insight, and confronted this

Rock who had been commissioned personally by Jesus to feed his lambs: "In spite of being a Jew, you live like the pagans and not like the Jews, so you have no right to make the pagans copy Jewish ways." (Gal. 2:14) The encounter, undoubtedly, was unpleasant, but Peter's humble openness and Paul's courage interacted for the good of the Christian community.

This passage shows how untrustworthy Peter was for the postion he held, how easily he was swayed by the presence of the "circumcision party." His dealings with the community in this situation were wavering and weak. Paul's action, painful though it must have been, sprang from fundamental trust. He did not trust in the validity or wisdom of Peter's action, nor in the rightness of his motivation. Seeing through these things, he put his trust on a deeper plane. He trusted that Peter, limited as he was, could still be open to the truth, admit his mistake and act accordingly. He trusted that his own conscience spoke the truth, and he acted upon it.

This is the kind of trust needed in any community. We are all fallible and weak. Sometimes our actions are unwise and our motivations are not pure, but we need others to believe that we can be open to the truth and able to grow once we see it. It takes courage to operate with this kind of trust. It can mean facing the superior with what appears to be favoritism or speaking to a friend about divulging privileged information. It does not mean that we have to suddenly become the conscience of the community, the truth-teller.

Building trust in community begins with myself. It means being open to the suggestions and criticisms of others, to the importance of praying and deliberating before I decide what to do, to bearing responsibility for my own insights, especially when they prove to be wrong. The openness I feel in myself sets the tone for trust in the community.

If I find that a person I trusted—for instance, someone in authority—revealed confidential information, my first response is naturally on the feeling level. Rightly I feel angry and hurt by this betrayal. "A person who holds a position of authority should respect the private communications of others and keep them confidential!"

Time passes and I am able to look at the situation more objectively. Is there anything I can do to build a more trusting atmosphere? Should I confront this person in a kind way and express how I really feel? Could it be that he is not aware of revealing my confidence?

I cannot undo what he has done nor can I decide never to speak to him again. Because of his position of authority, he will continue to play an important role in my life. This fact leads me to further reflection on my own inner attitudes.

God allowed this event to happen; though I find it hard to understand why—I still want to accept that God has chosen to test my trust in this way. Though I've been a victim of human weakness, the betrayal has taught me as never before the value of confidentiality in those in authority.

If and when I confront the person, another picture may emerge. I may find that from his perspective the act was construed not as a betrayal of trust but as a sharing of truth. He acted without realizing how I would feel, but in what he believed was the general interest.

Now I question whether I am making unrealistic demands for perfection. Can I allow for occasional mistakes on the part of those in leadership positions? Naturally, if trust is betrayed habitually, I must be cautious. What I do depends on the nature, severity, and frequency of the offenses.

Even if I need to be careful in divulging a confidence to another or in delegating responsibilities, I can still trust in their overall goodness and potential for growth in grace.

"What is expected of stewards is that each one should be found worthy of his trust," says St. Paul. (1 Cor. 4:2) If this requirement is lacking altogether, certainly I should do what is in my power to have the person replaced by one more qualified, without resorting myself to tactics that are untruthful, dishonest or unjust.

## II

## CONFLICT IN COMMUNITY

\* \* \*

The ideal of living our Christian commitment in community is often marred by either "submerged" or "open" conflict. Is there a way of handling these attitudes so that they do not destroy community but lead ultimately to strength and growth?

\* \* \*

If we want to understand the problem of conflict in community, we have to start by accepting the reality of conflict in our own lives. Think of the ambivalence we feel when we have to choose between two equally attractive possibilities.

A friend encourages me to vacation with him at his summer place; at the same time I am awarded a month long summer research grant. I feel torn between my need to relax after a trying school year and my desire to advance in my chosen field.

This ordinary human experience reminds us that ambivalence emerges out of interaction with the people and events that make up our daily world. To live is to be in conflict. It is to be faced with the challenge of choice. An array of attractions opens up before me and I realize sadly that I can never actualize all of them. Conflict reminds me of my human limitations. In saying *yes* to one possibility, I have to say *no* to others.

Since community is a collection of unique individuals, it follows that personal conflict will not cease. More likely than not, it will be intensified. My idea of what makes a good group often clashes with the vision another has. We may share a common goal, but chances are we approach it in different ways.

Conflict arises when we both insist that our way is the best one to implement the common good. Tempers flare. Misunderstandings arise and we feel discouraged.

The answer is not to pout in anger but to see what is happening as an opportunity for personal and communal growth. The deepest growth happens not when we resolve our differences, but when we remember that fundamentally our life in community depends on God's grace and on the constant cooperation of each of the persons living together.

While each of us has a unique gift to give, we must be willing to defer to the common good. Conflict tells us not to pack up and go away, but to become a reconciling presence, to remain in touch with our unique potential while bending toward peace with others.

How well we handle situations of conflict may be the test of our spiritual growth. For example, as a teacher, I advocate individualized instruction rather than direction of a whole class. Another teacher bitterly opposes this innovation. She has conducted a well disciplined seventh grade for years and is convinced that only in a structured situation can the teacher command respect. In my mind she seems always to be making little speeches for my benefit. I feel as if she is mocking my teaching methods. I feel threatened, but I push these negative emotions down, becoming increasingly upset as I try to avoid her as much as possible.

What can I do to handle this conflict? I could express my anger immediately, either by an explosive blow-up or by letting it seep through in the icy tones of my response. Neither of these solutions, however, would change her attitude. Even if I admit my angry feelings, patterns of politeness must be observed. The "silent treatment" is no solution either.

A more responsible answer might be to let go of my preoccupation with a new teaching method and wait until the opposition is less intense, less governed by feelings and more open to reason. I may fume in the privacy of my room, but later I will probably have to admit that there are also merits to the other teacher's method.

Perhaps compromise is possible to keep the peace in our small teaching community. Why let an overbearing or touchy attitude on either side threaten our commitment to the students? Perhaps in the future the topic can be discussed in a more open, less defensive way. For now we can cope with conflict without denying the possible truth of both positions. It is better to preserve the norms of courtesy and respect for the uniqueness of the other than merely to win a point.

It is impossible and even unhealthy to try to root out all conflict from community. Conflict is necessary for growth. A plant pushing through the hard-packed earth struggles against its environment to get the nourishment it needs. A child in conflict with his parents learns more about who he is. In fact some elements of conflict are essential to our spiritual self formation in that they spark autonomy and personal decision making.

Conflict is like a tension that results in action or reaction. Compare a sling shot. Too much tension breaks the elastic; too little makes it inefficient. This delicate balance is not easy to maintain. When conflict increases beyond the breaking point, I may try to repress it, but smoldering anger can become hazardous.

Burying feelings without any kind of insight or resolution only postpones or intensifies the issue. Submerging conflict is not the answer, but *how* and *when* does one bring it out in the open? *How* depends on my own sensitivity, on past experience, and on the graces I receive. *When* depends on my judgment, hopefully enlightened by the Holy Spirit, of the most appropriate opportunity to express what I am feeling.

Again we see the need for insight. If I am completely honest with myself, I may detect my own compulsive or resentful behavior. Then I can be more objective about the attitudes of others and reach beyond the immediacy of a situation to the good will inherent in every person. Prayerful recollection is always needed to deepen my receptivity to the light of the Holy Spirit.

Experience will tell me when our relationship is too brittle for confrontation or when the time is right for a frank discussion and a defusing of the tension.

To bring differences into the open involves risk. I may inadvertently hurt the other person by openly expressing my point of view. Though my intention is to do good, my action may result in pain or I may start out calmly enough but find my anger getting the best of me. Old accumulated angers may flare up. I'm shocked to find what a "slush fund" of animosity is bottled up inside. I end up losing control when all I wanted to do was reasonably express disagreement.

Expression of conflict can have positive results only if it flows from a deep source of love and concern for the other. Little traces of pettiness or hostility will signal destruction, whereas conflict that springs from honest disagreement can be an instrument of growth. If each member of the community longs for the transcendent good of the whole, conflict will not be reduced to back-biting or squabbling.

Knowing my own weakness before God generates gentleness and patience. This loving concern comes not from me but from Christ living in me. He said that he came to bring not only peace but the sword. (Mt. 10:34-36) Did he mean that conflict must necessarily result as we seek together to do the Father's will? Is he showing us that conflict can be a continual occasion for growth in compassion and grace?

## III

## DESTRUCTION OF COMMUNITY
## BY SPIRIT OF NEGATIVITY

\* \* \*

Is it possible that the wrong spirit of negativity could prevail and destroy a community? How can we best guard against negative attitudes?

\* \* \*

The uncharitable, the troublesome, the dissenters. We decry them and shake our heads in indignation. "What is going to happen to the community?" we ask.

I see the troublesome ones and sigh at the thought of having to live and work with them. "My life cannot be effective in such an atmosphere," I think. How can those who are uncharitable and disruptive of community be living a spiritual life? Do they draw their strength from diminishing one another? What is it that drives them on and elicits negativity?

Each of us has defects, but it is not these weaknesses that destroy a community. What destroys it is the failure of each member to live out his or her unique calling to union with Christ. The actual force of our presence to God counteracts the subtle traces of negativity, which the Evil Spirit uses to counteract the work of the Holy Spirit in a Christian community.

When a spirit of negativity prevails in a community, my first impulse is to blame rigid structures or to accuse the attitudes of the world of destroying the religious spirit. The truth is that a negative spirit abides in me, in each member of the community.

Think of the petty strife that exists in many communities—one group is closed off to the other, hurt feelings smart, cruel words are exchanged. If each member of a faction were searching sincerely for the will of God, differences of opinion could be powerful agents in promoting new life instead of contributing to mutual destruction.

Complaining and gossiping are highly infectious. They are a means of getting attention and of controlling others. Listening to little interesting details is part of the disease. Often we are eager for these tidbits of information and, of course, the most newsworthy are always negative.

When people feel a lack of excitement or challenge in their lives, they latch onto negative currents and augment them for their own sense of importance. It takes a conscious effort not to encourage what appear to be harmless remarks by either listening attentively to them or spreading them further.

When the light of the Holy Spirit invades my hardened heart, it prompts me to forgive others' hurtful deeds and cutting words. I do not double the problem by responding to negativity with more negativity. I try to take a positive approach: to see and do what is good; to operate less on the surface level of negativity and more from a source of quiet forgiveness and trust within.

It is the underlying presence of the Holy Spirit that motivates my spirit. This sustaining spirit is present in my responses to the people I meet everyday. Desire for intimacy with God encourages me to be more open so that the warmth of his Spirit becomes my own.

This Spirit protects me when other "spirits" take over within the community. I can deal with a noisy, nonrecollective atmosphere, obsessive work orientation, negligence in worship, or my own uncharitableness if I allow the Holy Spirit to temper my negative reactions with the grace of a truly Christian response.

Picture living in a situation where a person is greatly misunderstood and ill treated because she has not conformed to the "expected" behavior set by the group. Her approach to a task conflicts with "standard procedures" and consequently she is labeled "far out." She is criticized for being different, for not following the rules, for giving into personal whim. Lack of understanding could make her bitter, but she is mature enough to see beyond such gossip and does not go to pieces because of it. She believes that she is doing good work. As time goes on and she fails to fulfill the gossiper's predictions, people are able to accept her and even to give her encouragement and support. Rather than dragging herself down to the level of negative ridicule, she edifies others by her kindly response.

The "wrong spirit" is always deceptive and divisive. It thrives on gossip and gripes but soon dissolves if surrounded by good. This does not mean that every member of the community will become a model; it does mean that each person has to try, within her limits and shortcomings, to aim for the limitless goodness of living like Christ. He alone can turn the darkness to light and redeem us from the sins that divide our community.

Even the chronic complainer is a person pleading for understanding and love. His usual response is to continue to complain and cause heartache but beneath this dark exterior is a person longing for the light of Christ. He is the loving source that gives the good its strength to prevail over evil.

The spirit of Christian community is charitable because it is built on basis of each person's unique response to the call of the Holy Spirit in service of the common good. If I find myself becoming uncharitable, I know I am harboring a negative spirit. I need, then, to turn to the deeper spirit within me, to Christ who is the center of my life. Instead of reacting negatively to differences of opinion, I become gently aware of how people are suffering in my community, of what they are going through.

The essence of Christianity is to teach us the art of living compassionately. When we fall back into pettiness, gossip, willfulness, impatience, we forfeit the call to be another Christ and allow the negative spirit, the spirit of evil, to take over. This negative spirit diminishes both the person who harbors it and the one upon whom he vents himself; it can even be the basis of destruction of an entire community.

Though weakness and sin will always be mingled with our graced efforts to live Christ's suffering and love, it is only this compassion that can carry us forward. Only if we remain alive in God, will we be able to withstand the daily dyings that purify our hearts and promote growth in community.

*IV*

## *TRIVIA VS. TRUE VALUES IN COMMUNITY LIFE*

\* \* \*

How can the higher values of the spirit be lived in a community where non-essentials take precedence over personal creativity and spiritual deepening? How can we best deal with an emphasis on external appearance, cleanliness, rigidity of schedules to the neglect of personal-spiritual growth?

\* \* \*

The lot of the prophet is to be one who sees further than his companions. The first thing we need to be sure of is that our vision of the situation is right. Let's reflect on a biblical example.

When the Israelites complained about Moses' prolonged stay on Mount Sinai, it was because they were deprived not only of the comfort of his presence but of Yahweh's which was tangible for them through him. They built their golden calf much less out of wickedness than out of their strong desire to have a God they could see with their weak human eyes.

We all build golden calves that we are inclined to equate with God. We worship a clean house, duty, schedules, order and promptness. These are good things. We can see and control them. They gleam like gold in the here and now.

Cleaning house may be valued more highly than speaking to someone in need because it is a tidy, immediately rewarding project. Speaking to another has no neat boundaries, no built in reward. I can say to God, "I have done your will because I have cleaned this room perfectly," but who of us can say, "I have done your will because I have loved this person perfectly"?

Because we are all makers of golden calves, we need to feel compassion for one another. It was Moses' task to seize the golden calf, burn it, grind it into powder, and scatter the powder on the Israelites' drinking water. It is unlikely that we will be called to act with such thoroughness, but neither should we remain passive. We must not join in the worship of the community's golden calf, but, assured that we are assessing the situation objectively and softened by compassion, we can, when occasions arise, propose more relevant projects.

We can show that it is possible to be flexible and sociable and at the same time zealous and efficient. Then the way I clean house or come on time to community prayer can be used as an occasion, however minor, for spiritual deepening.

What if I am striving to live the deeper values of the spirit, whether or not other members of my community are doing likewise? Perhaps I have a special gift for getting to the heart of the matter rather than being caught up in the non-essentials. Not everyone has such a gift, which is why my personal presence can contribute much to this group. God may use me as a source of inspiration to others who are striving to live deeper values too.

It is not easy to stand alone, for community living ideally involves striving to restore common values. If my values are different, it may be painful to live them out; I may be tempted to give up what I believe in and to go along with the group simply not to feel alone.

Looked at from another angle, it may be that the values of those with whom I live are not so different from mine, but, because every person lives them out in a different way, they seem incompatible with my approach.

Thus I need to respect the way others live out their values while at the same time not surrendering my own. At times I may be harshly criticized. Others may see me as being careless in living my religious life while I think of myself as fostering creativity. They may misjudge my sensitivity to the needs of others as prying into their business. My way of praying may appear to them as superficial and sporadic while I may be trying honestly to follow the movements of the Spirit in my life.

What is it that can sustain me under this kind of criticism? Only my honest efforts to follow the Lord's call. As I discover day by day what he is asking of me and try to carry that out, I am at the same time growing deeper in my relationship with him. I should try also to grow in sensitivity to the feelings of others and in the art of not upsetting them unnecessarily by word or behavior.

We cannot deliberately change the living habits of those around us, but we may have an influence on them by our quiet faithfulness to the common life. Perhaps our life itself can say something to this group that no words could; we neither try to impose our convictions on others nor insist that they do things as we do; rather we try to be a silent witness to spiritual values for them.

Living community life implies respect for the gifts God gives to each member. In the Body of Christ, one person's weakness may be compensated for by another's strength. The person who is obsessed with cleaning probably keeps the house in good order. The one addicted to a schedule probably sees to it that meetings begin and end on time.

If we begin to think that exterior observance is the essence of community life, we may take on the attitude of the Pharisee who did all the right things but with an empty heart. He came before the Lord, grateful that he was not like the rest of men. Jesus denounced his way of presence and praised the way of the Publican. This man also fasted, contributed to the temple and prayed, but he came before the Lord as a sinner humbly begging for mercy. Jesus teaches us here that it is not what we do that counts but the attitude of heart with which we come to him.

We are not called to do certain things and then "pat ourselves on the back" because we have done them. We are always called to enter into the deeper levels of living, that is, to be motivated by love.

The higher values of the spirit do not exist in a cloud; they incarnate themselves in the simple, ordinary ways in which we live in the world with others. What more do we have than these little things to show our love and respect for the community?

To pour coffee in the morning, to be on time for a meal, to clean the house, to answer the telephone, to take someone to the doctor—all of these can be labeled "trivia" we have to get out of the way in order to get on to the "higher things of the spirit" or they can be transformed by loving hearts and hands. It is easy to get caught in the idea that the higher values must be expressed in heroic ways, whereas the truly heroic is usually hidden in the everyday routine.

St. Paul wrote in his Epistle to the Romans, "I cannot understand my own behavior. I fail to carry out the things I want to do, and I find myself doing the very things I hate." (Rm. 7:15) When we find ourselves caught up in busy work to the exclusion of being kind to others, we know what St. Paul means. We do not really intend to become so tied up with things that we are not available to people, but sometimes that happens despite our best intention.

We would rather not talk to someone because we are too busy. Perhaps the problem is that we spend lots of time concentrating on jobs that are safe because, unlike people, they are predictable. We fear the loss of security that comes when we venture into uncertain situations. Attempting to comfort others is much riskier than polishing a floor. There are many lonely people living in immaculately clean houses.

Life is made out of little things. The only way we can live our highest aspirations is by enfleshing them in day to day existence with our desire to love God and neighbor. There must be a growing unity between my highest spiritual ideals and my concrete moment-to-moment actions.

The little things of everyday life have to be the vessels that carry spiritual ideals; overwhelming details tend to lock us in a routinized existence that shields us from basic questions about the human condition.

We need humbly to esteem the everyday routines of life in which the richness of eternity enters the finiteness of the temporal. We need to keep them in their proper relationship to our central goal—to seek first the kingdom of God. In this process the Holy Spirit begins to cast the fire of his love into our hearts as the fear of our doubts is cast out.

## V

## *FEELING AT HOME*

**\* \* \***

Some people complain that they do not feel at home in
community because of a lack of understanding and love.
What can they do in such a situation?

**\* \* \***

A house can have an aura of warmth and love about it or
it can have a feeling of emptiness. I have been to a house
where I was welcomed; food and attention were given to
me, but still I felt ill at ease. What could be the reason for
such a feeling?

Often it is a nervousness, a feeling of ambivalence I
sense from my hosts. They make appropriate gestures, but
these are not accompanied with open sincerity. There is a
tenseness and lack of spontaneity in them.

The opposite is true of a host who is at home with
himself. Being at ease comes from a quiet confidence and
acceptance of self. A person has integrated both his gifts
and his flaws; his belief in himself permits humility. It requires confidence and humility to see one's petty, vain,
striving self and pray for help from God to accept this self
lovingly. This kind of trust in self, others and God produces ease and grace.

Thus when we are at home with ourselves, we can make
others feel at home. The atmosphere of such a community
is gracious. By contrast, when we are lacking in confidence
and gentle affirmation, we can unknowingly put others off
by our own inner ambivalence. They do not feel comfort-

able in our presence though we may be doing everything "technically" to make them feel at home.

Just as we must first love ourselves before we can love others, just as the unloved child is frightened of strangers, so the hesitant adult is anxious with outsiders. Anxious or gracious—it all goes back to our sense of self worth.

What are the ingredients that go into being at home? They are security and a sense of belonging. Home, above all else, represents protection—a place where we can retreat from the trials of the outside world. For example, a student can feel at home in the modest quarters he occupies during his college years. Books, papers, typewriter, a stray coffee cup or two—all attest to the fact that this simple room is his dwelling.

This contented feeling accompanies him when he leaves the room to follow his daily schedule because he knows he has a home to come back to. Attending classes, lunching with friends or fellow students, jostling with the crowd intent upon catching the bus—none of these activities robs him of his feeling of going home. He knows that part of this feeling has to do with a sense of security in his daily situation. Yet he cannot say that the physical situation in which he finds himself constitutes this feeling entirely. There is something deeper.

He recalls being with his friends one evening. The apartment was alive with spirited conversation. He contributed to the give and take—noticing the warm blend of silence and speech, of listening and responding, of being present to the others and to himself. "Being at home," he thought, "is to be with one another." For all of us, it is the hum of friendly conversation, the smell of good cooking, the warm feeling of being friends together.

In the warm shelter of such personal experiences, I find a kind of plentitude of life. Feeling at home is not an emotion to define but an aura of familiarity, a sense of things fitting together, of belonging, of harmony and order.

The home our parents provided for us as infants, the feelings of warmth and security we experienced there, are forever models for our future homes. This original shelter is essential for our survival and we never outgrow our need for it.

While the security of home can provide relaxation and refreshment, it can point also to a negative desire for a tepid and complacent life. Home can make me feel so comfortable that I refuse to meet further challenges; it can cause a kind of fossilization whereby I take my life for granted and all that comes into it.

In this frame of mind, I can make home merely a secure nook of togetherness and support out of which the true challenge of love has been drained. I close myself off from the dying to self-centered needs that is involved in true love—the dying that implies being misunderstood and having my ideas rejected from time to time.

Shoulder to shoulder with other human beings, I am bound to encounter failure; I am not going to accept everyone easily or be accepted by all. I am going to encounter some rejection no matter how loving a community is.

I may have unrealistic expectations of community life, seeking deeply fulfilling relationships without the inevitable suffering that goes with love. When these expectations are not met, I may feel compelled to leave and seek the "idol of warm togetherness" elsewhere. But that "elsewhere" never comes. Rejection and misunderstanding are part of the human condition. No change of residence will alter this fact.

As a Christian, I should be able to see that all genuine life comes through death. Often the feeling of being at home comes only after I pass through the crucible of alienation, disharmony and non-acceptance. Even when there is turmoil all around me, I can still experience a sense of inner peace. If I do not feel quiet within, then no matter what anyone does to make me feel at home it will not change my discomfort.

When I am at home within myself, I am at rest; I find it right to be the person I am. With God's loving care, I can accept myself. And so, while many things seem to be falling apart around me, I am at rest and at home, for the Son of God himself lives in me and allows me to be who I am.

"Foxes have holes and the birds of the air have nests, but the Son of Man has nowhere to lay his head." (Lk. 9: 58) That saying always strikes a plaintive chord in us. Christ seems to be declaring that he has no earthly home, that many will reject him, that men will not allow him to make his home in them. What message is he giving us in these haunting words: " . . . but the Son of Man has nowhere to lay his head."

Christ stayed at Peter's house. He was completely at home there. Days later, while the disciples were rocking back and forth, afraid for their lives in a terrible storm, Jesus lay sound asleep in the boat. He is at home in the storm too. Often he spent time in the house of his friends Martha, Mary and Lazarus where he was very much at ease. He seemed to be at home *everywhere* and yet *nowhere* in particular, for strangely enough, when disciples ask if they can follow him, he warns them that he has nowhere to lay his head, as if that will be their lot as well.

How hard, in this light, should I search for the perfect sense of being at home? At times Jesus was rejected in his home country of Nazareth. He wept for a Jerusalem that turned away from him. He suffered abandonment and denial by his apostles when he needed them the most.

As the Son of Man, he had no one place he could call home, no one place he could continually return to. But he had peace and was at home with himself because of his union with his Father. He had come to do his will and then, as Son of God, he would return to his Father's house.

It seems that Christ's warning that he has nowhere to lay his head is a reminder not to search for the perfect home here on earth. We must pass through the crucible of earthly limits into that joyous homecoming that lies beyond the present life. We must let go of our emotional need for that idealized place. We must be careful not to attach too much significance to harmonious togetherness.

The way of Christ, the Son of God and Man, is one that leads to the Father's house and that is the only shelter we Christians must ultimately seek.

## VI

## FRIENDSHIP IN THE SPIRITUAL LIFE

\* \* \*

What role does friendship play in the spiritual life? Is it a help or a hindrance in our quest for union with God?

\* \* \*

A true friend is a gift beyond price. Friendship cannot be forced. Like happiness, it may come to us as an unexpected blessing.

As we journey through life, there are many obstacles that block God's grace. Our selfishness may keep people at a distance and especially the Lord. We become preoccupied with our own universe. We trust no one and move about as if we were our own savior. These obstacles can be tempered when we are with a true friend, for friendship calls us out of ourselves. As we allow another to share our world, as we live in his, we transcend the narrow confines of self.

As we begin to feel comfortable with our friend, we also begin to feel more at one with ourselves. If the friendship is a healthy one, each of us becomes strengthened to stand on his own feet. I know that my life is seen as valuable by the other person, whose respect and love fill me with gratitude. What better climate of heart can there be for union with God?

When I am with my friend, we can often sense the presence of God between us. Like the disciples on the road to Emmaus, our friendship can be the occasion in which Jesus joins us in a special way. In the face of discouragement, these two disciples remained together. They had given up everything and fled, but they had not given up each other. When they held firm to their human relationship, even though all their dreams and hopes were apparently shattered, the God they considered to be so far off was near.

Through this touching story, Jesus may be telling us to hold fast to those friendships that come our way. The difficulties we encounter in relationship with a friend can teach us much about ourselves and the ways in which we can become more intimate with the other.

When I first find a friend, I may be overjoyed at the many things we share in common. It seems as if we are made of the same "stuff." Our friendship nourishes us and affirms the persons we are. As the friendship begins to develop, I begin to be called forth by the other in a new way. Disagreements may arise between us. I begin to see faults and weaknesses and I feel disappointed.

There seem to be real obstacles in our relationship. Many times I may think one of these stumbling blocks is "the beginning of the end," but it is really just a beginning. As I work through each of these obstacles with my friend, I find that the relationship grows stronger, not weaker. I find that I care now in a less selfish way. It is part of human nature to be possessive of the other person at times.

As I work through difficulties in the relationship, I slowly become purified of this tendency. I grow in true respect and care for the other. My love becomes more and more purified.

Growing in relationship with a friend can thus teach us much about growing in relationship with God. When we first meet God in a personal way, we are infatuated with the promise of fulfillment. We sense somehow that we shall find perfect happiness if we continue on this road to him. And we are right. But there are obstacles along the way too. The difference in this case is that all the obstacles are not in him but in us. As we work through these hindrances, however, we become purified in our love for God and slowly enter into a deeper union with him.

Relationship with a friend can teach us not only to be more thoughtful, trusting and caring; it can also help us become more open. This openness, which is an allowing the other to be just as he is, can teach us to grow in openness to God. We allow him to really be God in our life, making ourselves more ready to respond to the movements of his grace wherever they lead.

Regarding this point, a poster reads: "A friend sees you through even when he sees through you." A friend is someone with whom I can talk about things that really concern me. I don't have to be afraid of saying something stupid or foolish. I don't have to try to be eloquent or impressive. If I did, my friend could see through the ploy anyway.

With my friend, I don't have to be someone I am not in order to be liked. I can be the imperfect self I am. I feel affirmed. This affirmation does not lead me to become embedded in what I am right now. Friendship helps me to grow from there.

My friend sees me through—through a bad mood, a trying experience, through something about which we have disagreed. I may feel his support in kind words, through a helping hand, a concerned confrontation, a stimulating argument. My friend sees me through to what I can become—no matter how slowly I stumble along.

An obstacle to grace is the burden I place on myself by feeling that I must make myself worthy of God's love, that I must earn his favor. I feel as if I have to be perfect. If I make a mistake or fail, I fall into disfavor. I become tense and anxious. I am alone in my striving. I feel I have to make it so that I can *get* God's grace. Such willfulness has no place here. Grace is a gift. It is a pure gift before I do anything. While I am wholly unworthy, God is present to me in my imperfection. His love embraces me even when I am unfaithful or forgetful.

God's grace works through who I am now. It does not lie in wait until I become who I would like to be or should be. All I need is an attitude of receptivity—to accept humbly his presence.

The graciousness of God can be overwhelming. It can be too much for me to take. The whole atmosphere in which I live says I have to compete for what I get. I have to earn it. I find it difficult to experience pure gift.

Although it is a faint image, my relationship with my friend reflects something of my relationship with God. God sees through me perfectly. He sees me as I can never see myself—in all my superficiality and weakness—yet his vision goes beyond to my deepest center. Even though I am far from that image he has made, God sees me through.

Friendship can thus be a facilitating condition for spiritual growth. A friend can open my eyes to the beauty of others and to my own special gifts as well as help me to become more aware of my blind spots. In the pain that is part of any true relation, I can learn generosity, other-centeredness, compassion—how to love another in the real world as an imperfect, limited being.

A close friendship can call me to greater detachment if I allow the other to fulfill the mystery of his unique calling, no matter how much I desire him to be with me. If I am without a close friend, this situation need not send me on a panicky search for deep interaction; it can be a call to grow through solitude closer to God and more sensitive to others. If I am blessed with a friendship I need to remain conscious of its finite character against the ultimate horizon of my love for God.

Spiritual friendship can strip away many obstacles to my relationship with God, provided my love and desire for God increases with my affection for my friend. Only then can the friendship be a truly spiritual one. My friend and I need to be aware of the limited nature of human friendship and desirous of holding our hearts for the love that lasts through this life and into the next, claiming and giving absolutely everything.

True friendship helps to bring out the "flaws" of each other's personality that keep us from being our best selves. For example, I need to have the final say in every situation; my friend helps me to be sure of the abilities I do have but also to admit where I am limited. Or I find it difficult to communicate with certain individuals; my friend helps me to appreciate the different talents of these people and eventually learn to be open to them.

When friendship is purified by a common goal to live in union with Christ, it helps me interact in a far richer way with those with whom I live and work. In the words of Antoine Saint-Exupery, "Love does not consist in gazing at each other . . . but in looking outward together in the same direction."